COMPLETE
RAILWAY
MODELLING

COMPLETE RAILWAY Modelling

EDITED BY VIC SMEED

CHILTON BOOK COMPANY

Preceding pages: Detailed look at a hand-built steam locomotive in 0 scale by Robert Whelove.

Above: A Hornby train set of the early 1920s of the type that led to an increasing interest in railway modelling.

Published by Ebury Press
National Magazine House
72 Broadwick Street
London   W1V 2BP

Second Impression   1982

Printed and bound by
TONSA, San Sebastian, Spain

First published in the United States of America in 1983 by Chilton Book Company, Radnor, Pennsylvania 19089, and simultaneously in Canada by Fleet Publishers, a Division of International Thomson Limited, 1410 Birchmount Road, Scarborough, Ontario M1P 2E7

Library of Congress Catalog Card No. 82–73546

ISBN 0–8019–7367–8

CONTENTS

FOREWORD

Models and miniatures have held a fascination for man since time immemorial, and examples of small boats and chariots, often made in clay, have survived some 5,000 years from the Cretan, Sumerian and Ancient Egyptian civilizations in evidence. Railways, too, go back further than many people realise, since 2,000 years ago the Romans evolved a form of paved railway system for beast-drawn wagons. Developments of the same basic idea occurred from about 300 years ago in, particularly, the mining areas of north-east England, where horse-drawn waggons (two 'g's in these days!) transported coal from mines to ship-loading staithes on the rivers.

Mechanically-propelled models of wheeled vehicles became commercially available in the latter part of the 19th century and over the years grew in sophistication and fidelity to the prototypes on which they were loosely based, but it was not until the 1920s and '30s that huge strides were made in popularity.

Early model railways demanded a con-siderable amount of space and were a little beyond the financial resources of the average family, especially since the between-war depression affected a majority of people in the developed countries. However, prices were steadily reducing and the introduction of smaller gauges opened the possibilities of layouts in the average home. The wide commercial target was boys and by the late 1930s the average boy had some experience of model trains and many discovered a life-long hobby.

Innovation, increasing technology and the ever-growing sophistication of customers' demands have brought us today to a multi-faceted international hobby and, inevitably, specialisation into particular areas of interest by its exponents.

This book, with the help of a number of well-known contributors, sets out both to extend that appreciation and outline knowledge to the reader, and to provide more detailed accounts of the areas common to all specialist fields.

CONTRIBUTORS

Denis Moore
Familiar with all types and sizes of layouts Denis Moore is a respected contributor to model magazines.

Cyril Freezer
Former editor of *Railway Modeller*, now editor of *Model Railways* and a prolific writer on all aspects of railway modelling.

Nelson Twells
A well known writer on practical model railway subjects for many years Nelson Twells is associated with several major English clubs and modelling exhibitions.

Don Townsley
A leading locomotive expert and chairman of one of the largest model railway societies.

Harry Drummond
An acknowledged expert on most aspects of railways, Harry Drummond is particularly known for his expertise on rolling stock.

Peter Gomm
A practical but authoritative enthusiast of many years' standing, Peter Gomm is known for his collection of early model railway equipment.

Rolf Ertmer
Professional photographer and writer of German model railway magazine, Rolf Ertmer is famous for his layout 'Altenbeken'.

Robert Hegge
Professional photographer and contributor to *American Railroad Modeller*; Robert Hegge is known for his 'Crooked Mountain Lines' layout.

Produced by
Garratt Allen Edwards Limited

Art Direction and Co-ordination
Terry Allen

Design
Richard Garratt

Text Editor
Carole Edwards

Illustration
Terry Allen Designs Limited/
Lyn D. Brooks Roger Courthold
R. W. Stoneman.

Photography and Scenery,
unless credited otherwise
John Wylie

Preceding pages: A rarity from an early Trix programme, the 'Adler' (Eagle).

Left: H0 is one of the most common track sizes used, the scale of which can be clearly seen in this photograph.

SCALES, SPACE & SELECTION

Many people are introduced to the hobby of railway modelling by the gift of a boxed train set. This usually consists of a locomotive, two or three coaches or goods wagons and a simple oval track in sections. Although initially enjoyable, this set has very limited scope and the operator will soon be keen to extend the track and develop the layout further. The purpose of this book is to help the beginner to achieve the satisfaction of creating a model railway from his basic, commercially-packaged train set.

Much interest can be found in the construction aspect: building the baseboard, laying and wiring the track and providing buildings and natural scenery. Beautifully authentic buildings and accessories are available in kit form and the very keen modellers will even try designing and making their own. Part of the appeal of railway modelling as a hobby is the creation of realistic layouts and with the advent of plastic injection moulding and other techniques, tiny details of the prototype can be reproduced on the smallest scale.

The photograph on the far left shows an assortment of 'tinplate' 7mm 0 gauge railway vehicles and scenic accessories. In the background is an example of early three-rail electric track, contrasted with a modern 00 set of much smaller size and greater sophistication shown above.

The very first model train was made in Germany during the 1830s. This was a push-along toy engine with no means of propulsion and no rails or track. One of the earliest model steam locomotives was built by the father of Sir Henry Wood, conductor and founder of the Promenade Concerts. Although actually powered by steam, it is believed that no track was available. This was quickly followed by German model locomotives fired by a methylated spirit burner which heated a water-filled boiler. The steam drove the model via an oscillating cylinder. Such models were known as 'dribblers' or 'piddlers' for obvious reasons and were quite large models by today's standards, being approximately what is now known as gauge 1. During the 1880s clockwork mechanisms were fitted into the engines, which proved much safer than the early steam-powered toys which virtually had no means of control. By the 1890s a form of sectioned track was introduced by Marklin, a German company which is still very prominent in the model railway industry today.

Another notable German manufacturer was Bing, who made gauge 0 tin-plate models powered by clockwork. With an eye to expanding business by both parties, they entered into an agreement with an English manufacturer, W. J. Bassett-Lowke of Northampton, and in 1901 began to produce tinplate models of British outline trains. This arrangement continued until the 1930s, except for an obvious break during the hostilities of 1914–18.

The United States were also producing train sets, mainly of USA outline in 0 and standard gauges, made by a firm called Lionel. The Lionel Co. was founded in New York in 1901 when Joshua Lionel Cowan built his first $2\frac{7}{8}$in gauge models. In 1906 he marketed the Standard gauge using $2\frac{1}{4}$in track. These were built until the start of the Second World War, being listed in the 1942 catalogue. Lionel first produced 0 gauge trains in 1915 using a measure of $1\frac{1}{4}$in between the rails. This gauge is the only one produced today.

In 1910, the first Ives 0 gauge trains left the factory in Bridgeport, Conn. In 1918, the factory produced gauge 1 types. These were dropped in the early 1920s when Ives brought out the Standard gauge models in 1925. Ives' factory closed in 1929 but Lionel continued building trains using Ives' dies in the early 1930s.

American Flyer Co. began in 1907 but it was not until fifteen years later that an 0 gauge 4-4-4 electric train was produced with more than four wheels. The firm had built clockwork and electric models of the smaller size in the early days.

In 1925, American Flyer brought out their Standard gauge models. It was the last company in America to produce the larger size which the company called 'wide gauge'. These were dropped in 1929. Later A. C. Gilbert manufactured American Flyer trains in 0 gauge and marketed S gauge between 1945 and 1966. In 1979 Lionel produced three cars made from the old American Flyer dies. In 1980, Lionel produced three more cars. No new engines have been manufactured in S gauge since 1966. The cars made by Lionel are all in S gauge ($\frac{7}{8}$in between rails or $\frac{3}{16}$in : 1ft).

In 1924, Julius and Milton Forcheimer of Newark, New Jersey, marketed their popular Dorfan trains and pioneered the use of die castings. They built 0 gauge clockwork types and 0-4-0 electric types. Standard gauges were also brought out and while the trains were very well-made, containing new construction features, the firm closed down in the late 1920s. Today, only Lionel is still successfully building equipment in the 0 gauge for American enthusiasts.

By the early 1920s, electric motors were being widely used as an alternative to clockwork, the motor usually powered from accumulators giving a supply of 6-volt DC. The current was fed to a centre rail, placed between the running tracks. It was picked up by a spoon-shaped collector underneath the locomotive.

After the end of the First World War, Frank Hornby, the inventor of Meccano, launched his Hornby Trains in 1920. These tinplate, gauge 0 models, which were entirely British made, had a remarkable impact on the model train market and quite soon swept away most of the foreign imports. Both clockwork and electrically-propelled trains were available. Within a few years a large range of locomotives, coaches, wagons and accessories had been produced, all to a high standard and with a very fine enamelled finish on the tinplate.

Gauge 0 had by this time become the established size and while Hornby made for the 'man-in-the-street' and the younger enthusiast, other firms such as Bassett-Lowke, Mills Brothers and the Leeds Model Company produced more up-market models which were nearer scale, with accessories and products for the discerning enthusiast.

During the 1930s several keen model railway enthusiasts, who made everything themselves, were building models half the size of the gauge 0 ones, and this became known as 'Half 0' or H0. It was taken up commercially, being produced by Bing and marketed by Bassett-Lowke, and known as the Table Top Railway; however, for some inexplicable reason it never proved as popular as its sponsors hoped and had a very short life. Later it was resurrected but instead of the models being exact Half 0 or 3.5mm : 1ft scale, they were made to a scale of 4mm : 1ft. This was because there were difficulties in getting the electric motors into the smaller outline British locomotives, which have a smaller loading gauge than those of the Continent or America. This new size was known as 00 gauge (16.5mm between rails) and is the most popular size today.

Commercially it was again Frank Hornby who led the way for others when he introduced his Hornby Dublo trains in 1938, which in a space of one year gained great momentum until halted by the outbreak of the Second World War. Both clockwork and electric train sets and locomotives were available, although after the war only the electrically-powered ones were produced.

Another venture into the smaller scales was made by Trix of Germany, who introduced their Trix Twin system. This was H0 gauge and electrically-powered, but with a difference—Trix had developed a simple system whereby the centre rail was positive and the two running rails were negative. Thus it was possible to run two trains simultaneously and independently on the same track, one being fed with current from the centre and left-hand rail, while the other was fed from the centre and the right-hand rail.

With the advent of the war in 1939 all production of model railways virtually ceased and when the trade recommenced in 1946–47 several changes were apparent, the foremost being the almost universal appeal of the smaller 00 gauge. This quickly ousted 0 gauge and Hornby Dublo became firmly established. In 1951 a small firm, Rovex Plastics, who were producing cheap 00 gauge train sets for a departmental store, was purchased by the Tri-ang Group and they made great strides in developing mass-produced model railway equipment, finally purchasing Hornby in 1965 and producing Tri-ang Hornby Railways. The range continued to expand and attain better standards and detail, but in 1972 the parent company ran into financial difficulties and was purchased by Dunbee Combex-Marx Ltd. The Tri-ang trade mark having been sold to another group

A clockwork mechanism from a Bassett-Lowke locomotive of the 1930s. The levers protruded into the cab and were pushed for forward or reverse running. Note the absence of flanges on the centre wheels, to facilitate negotiation of non-scale small radius curves.

meant that the model railways had now to be called Hornby, although by this time the original influence of Frank Hornby and Hornby Dublo had long since ceased. To complicate the story, Wrenn were producing a range of models using the old Hornby Dublo moulds. The name Hornby was once again a brand name, as it remains today, although a further financial setback has meant that the parent company is now in liquidation.

In the mid-70s two well-established firms entered the 00 gauge model railway market and today their products are much respected. The first was Airfix, known for many years as a producer of plastic kits, toys and household utensils. Their railway products were produced in Hong Kong, although designed and tooled in this country. They can now offer a complete system and a wide variety of locomotives and rolling stock, both passenger coaches and freight wagons of a very high standard. The other company was Palitoy (part of the American-owned General Mills Corporation) who are producing model railway equipment under the trade name Mainline. Again actually produced in Hong Kong, the models quickly became popular and established the firm in this new field. Fortunately, the products of these three major manufacturers—Hornby, Airfix and Palitoy—are compatible in all respects, so there is no trouble in inter-mixing the products of one with the other.

Since the mid-50s there has been a tremendous growth in the number of small firms who are producing model railway accessories and kits of parts enabling the enthusiast to make his own locomotives, coaches etc.

In the early 1960s a West German firm, Arnold, introduced N gauge models which are approximately half the size of 00 gauge. This found almost instant appeal on the Continent and was quickly followed by many other firms manufacturing in this scale. The production of English outline models was slow, but there is now a moderate selection available, aided by the British firm of Graham Farish, who at one time produced 00 gauge but are now almost exclusively devoted to N gauge. Peco is another firm who produce wagons and accessories for the smaller size.

The well-established firm of Marklin produced the smaller Z gauge models in 1972, but they are the only manufacturer in this size at the present time. They are all Continental, mainly German outline models, although at the time of writing, plans are being made for one of the smaller English firms to produce some die-cast British outline bodies to fit the Marklin chassis and motors.

Gauge 0 still has a healthy following, but it does require a lot of space in the modern home, and of course it is more expensive. It is, however, ideal for the garden layout.

In recent years there has been an increase in the interest shown in Narrow Gauge railways—probably due to the efforts made with the preservation of some of the old quarry and industrial railways such as the Festiniog and Talyllyn Railways in North Wales and others scattered around the British Isles. Modelling the narrow gauge railways will enable one to have a comparatively small layout, yet one that will have the atmosphere of the prototype. It is pointless to try and portray the line from Paddington to the Devon coast in a space of say, 20ft × 15ft—even in N gauge, where a prototypical 13 coach main line train will have a length of about 7ft 6in (230cm). The locomotive would arrive at the terminal station before the last coach has cleared the end of the platform of the starting station! Of course, there are ways of overcoming this problem, such as running the train round a series of loops etc., but the general overall impression is a poor compromise and unless very skilfully disguised will have a toy-like appearance. Narrow gauge, on the other hand, usually has a simple prototype track plan, and the modeller can use a larger scale for the rolling stock and the scenery, yet have the smaller size for the track gauge. A popular scale is known as 009 (or 00n9) which is 4mm scale for the rolling stock and buildings, but runs on N gauge track. Smaller radius curves can be accommodated and trains are usually only five or six short four-wheeled coaches. Train operation is relatively simple, and the construction of realistic scenery usually plays an important role for the modeller of the narrow gauges. Several firms produce kits to fit on proprietary chassis etc. It is not only the smaller sizes that exist for narrow gauge, as the German firm of LGB (Lehmann Garten Bahn) produces some plastic models of Continental narrow gauge prototypes to run on gauge 1 track. They are, as the title suggests, ideal for the garden railway.

With the shortage of suitable space in

the modern house, the garden railway has come into its own. The large LGB system mentioned above is ideal, and so is gauge 0; even gauge 00 is quite capable of being operated in the garden, although of course the smaller the scale, the greater the problem of dealing with fallen leaves, bits of earth and insects etc. With the vast range of 'Do-it-Yourself' aids now available it is a simple matter to waterproof wood, make concrete, etc. and so make a good support or form a waterproof and rot-resisting track bed.

The garden railway also has the advantage that live steam propulsion can be enjoyed in safer circumstances than in the house. There are several live steam models now available for gauge 1 (which can be coal-fired) and spirit or butane gas burning

locos for gauge 0. The former can be very expensive but the latter does have more reasonably priced models available. We have even seen and tested a 00 gauge locomotive fired by butane gas, the steam entering a small oscillating cylinder. This was most impressive in such a small scale, but of course, control of such a model is not easy, and it is not such a practical proposition to have a large layout all powered by such small live steam locomotives. It is also doubtful if there is yet enough demand for mass produced models, but with technical advances it could be commonplace in ten years.

The normal method of propulsion is by electric motor and during the 1939–45 War great progress was made in the manufacture of more powerful and smaller

Similar locomotives in 1, H0 and Z gauge give some idea of the enormous variation between the largest and the smallest of the 'electric gauges'. The engines are all from Marklin and are based on the German Class 80 0-6-0 side-tank locomotive.

magnets, which in turn have been applied, together with other technology, in the improvement of small motors. Many of the motors in the scale models today are manufactured in Switzerland, West Germany or Japan, and these motors are extremely powerful, quiet and reliable. The standard current is 12-volt DC and there is a wide variety of controllers on the market to operate such motors. These vary from the simple variable resistance type to the more advanced electronic controllers which give ultra smooth control, will give greater power for locos proceeding up a gradient, and hold it back running down the grade, thus keeping a more constant speed and giving greater realism.

In 1978 both Hornby and Airfix introduced a totally new concept in model railway control systems. This is the two-wire or command control, which utilises an electronic micro-chip in the model and by giving certain coded signals superimposed on top of the normal track voltage the loco will respond to the transmitted message. It is possible to run up to four locos independently on the same track, and to change points etc., by merely pushing a button. Hornby have called their system Zero-1, while the Airfix system is known as Multiple Train Control. It is clearly too early to evaluate the impact of these revolutionary systems on the model railway market, but no doubt in a few years' time this system, or a modification of it, will be generally accepted. There is however, a word of warning, for at the moment both systems work on 20-volt AC and are not compatible with each other. Further, they will only accept a model fitted with one of their chips and there is a strong possibility that a normal 12-volt loco will burn its motor out if placed on the track of a system fitted with command control. Similarly, a loco fitted with a chip will not operate on a conventional 12-volt controller-operated layout.

Possibly as a result of the increased overseas business travel, or the popular concept of taking holidays abroad, or merely the fact that Continental railways are different and colourful, many more enthusiasts are turning to modelling the railways of mainland European countries, and layouts depicting the French SNCF (Société Nationale des Chemins de Fer) or the West German DB (Deutsches Bundesbahn) are now quite common in other countries. Certainly one of the attrac-

tions of modelling the Continental railways is the reliability of the models and the vast amount of small detail which is incorporated into the mouldings etc., at which the Continental manufacturers seem to excel, and they make scale models with no concession to the toy trade. Most of the manufacturers' products are readily available in H0 and N scales, the major producers in H0 being Jouef (France), Fleischmann, Trix, Liliput, Marklin, and Roco (all West German), Peco (East German) and Lima and Rivarossi (Italian). In N gauge there is Arnold, Minitrix and Fleischmann (all West German). All these manufacturers present a vast range of locomotives and rolling stock as well as accessories, not confining themselves to the prototypes of their own country; thus there are models available to cover the whole of Europe. With the number of trains running between two or more countries, it is normal to see coaches of one country in another. There are also many manufacturers on the Continent who specialise in scenic items and plastic building kits e.g. Faller, Heljan, Kibri, Pola, Vollmer etc.

Reference has already been made to the difference between British 00 and H0 scales and the Continental and American modeller who works to H0 scale which is accurate to the track gauge—3.5mm : 1ft scale and the track gauge of 16.5mm, or a ratio of 1 : 87. Thus H0 scale coaches look smaller than the British 00, even though their full size counterparts are larger. The difficulty of getting electric motors into the smaller body size of the British locomotive has also made a difference to N scale, so while both English and Continental run on 9mm track, the former is to a ratio of 1 : 148 while our friends across the Channel (including America) use a ratio of 1 : 160.

In most European countries there are now many hundreds of miles of main line electrified with the overhead system, and thus the electric locomotives are all fitted with pantographs to collect the current from the overhead wire. Nearly all the models of such locomotives also have a working pantograph and by turning a small switch, often hidden underneath the model, or disguised as an insulator on the roof, the current can be changed from pick-up via the running rails or via the overhead. Model catenary is also available from the Continental manufacturers, and, of course, it is possible to run two items of motive power independently on the same track—one working from the overhead and one from the track.

Many modellers favour portraying the American scene and here again the chosen scale is either H0 or N (Continental size or ratio). The models of American steam out-line locos are dominated by the ready-to-run brass replicas from Japan or Korea and are expensive by the time they reach the English shores, although they are superb models. Rivarossi (Italy), Mechanotechnica (Jugoslavia) and Bachmann (USA) produce both steam and diesel outline locos and Athearn (USA) diesel only. The rolling stock for the American market is mainly the province of kits, or more accurately 'knocked-down-for-packing' models, which only need a minimal amount of tools and time to assemble. Many wooden kits are available in America, from the old time coaches to lineside building kits and these are all very good, the wood being ready cut and shaped and often the scoring of indivi-dual planking is already carried out.

Both Continental and American layouts will give greater scope for scenic modelling as their lines traverse mountains, gorges and rivers of vast proportions, unlike any-thing in the British Isles. Such scenic modelling can be most effective with the smaller N gauge layouts, which allow much more space for such items.

Whichever prototype one chooses to model, one must always remember that a scene cannot accurately be portrayed in which there are anomalies with the period involved. For example, it is no use having a model of a pre-Nationalisation locomotive such as a Great Western Railway 'Castle' class hauling a train of the latest British Rail coaches.

Thought must also be given to the realistic operation of a model railway, for running trains aimlessly round and round soon becomes boring, and one is not obtaining the full benefits and value of the hobby. Timetable running is of consider-able interest in two different ways. First, the planning of the timetable can tax the ingenuity of the layout owner or chief operator. In much the same way as the full size railways have to cope with trains that deal solely with the rush-hour traffic and fit in excursions and specials and so on, all this can be recreated in miniature. The compilation of the timetable, using a speeded up clock, can baffle the brains of the finest administrator. It is even more taxing for the operators who have to run the trains to the prescribed timetable, especially if minor breakdowns or derail-ments occur, which may cause single line working. The maxim should be that the trains must be kept running, so that imagination and ingenuity can play their part in endeavouring to keep the service in operation and restrict the inevitable delays to a minimum. To add to the enjoyment one can try and work in a special VIP train without disrupting the timetable. This is a dodge that the 'controller' can try and use to bewilder and fluster his operators!

There is plenty of scope for all interests in the model railway hobby whether it be carpentry for the baseboards, metal work in making locomotives and rolling stock, electrical work for the wiring and control gear, artistic work for scenery and back-grounds, or the pure administrative powers for the compilation of a timetable.

It is the collection of such experts which makes the success of the model railway clubs and societies which exist up and down the country, on the Continent and in America. Membership of a club will give the modeller a much deeper insight into the wonders of model railways and will further his education.

There are currently about a dozen different scales that come within our sphere, from the smallest Z gauge to gauge 1; above that the larger sizes really fall within the category of model engineer-ing and are usually the domain of the live steam brigade, although there are some models which are large enough to haul passengers and are powered by miniature diesel engines.

There are, of course, some specialist scales for which the trade do not cater and in these cases many of the components have to be made by the individual. In recent years there has been a greater demand for exact scale for both track and models, thus the formation of the Protofour and Scalefour Societies in the United Kingdom, which are exact scale versions of the popular 00 gauge, the difference being that whereas the 00 gauge enthusiast can walk into a model shop and find materials and stock to suit his requirements, the true scale person may have to order from a specialist firm or make his own, and con-sequently such tools as lathes are far more important.

Brief details of the now generally accepted scales and gauges are listed on page 178.

TRACK DESIGN

It is almost certain that your first introduction to model railways comes through the purchase or gift of an attractively boxed set containing just enough equipment for operation—a locomotive, either steam or diesel, with some coaches or wagons and a selection of track. The track usually comes in eight curved and two or four straight sections which, when clipped together, form an oval track around which the assembled train will endlessly chase its tail, clockwise for a while and then, at the whim of the owner, anticlockwise.

The need for more varied operating facilities very soon makes itself felt, often in the form of a preoccupation with arranged crashes and collisions! So additional trackage, points or turn-outs and crossings (switches and diamonds) are obtained, thus making possible the construction of loops and sidings. Wagons can now be shunted from siding to siding and additional locomotives can be accommodated, isolated in loops or spur sidings, to be brought on to the main circuit in turn with goods or passenger trains.

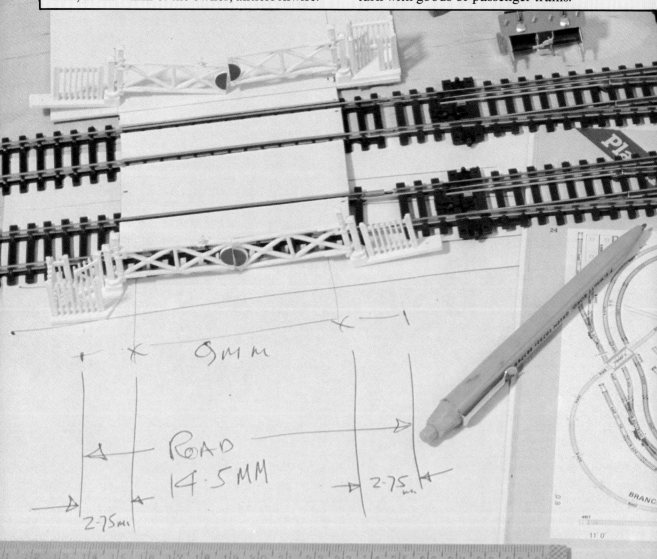

Variations of track layout are often tried at this stage. Many manufacturers' catalogues illustrate layout schemes, often with a list of the reference numbers and quantities of each item that are required. In this way, the exact amount of track is known and can be purchased to suit the layout of your choice, within, naturally, the personal restraints of price and space. In any case, studying catalogues is a fascinating pastime in its own right as you picture the various paths that the trains can take over the layout. You will become familiar with the sort of operation that is possible with different arrangements, and it is almost inevitable that variations of the set schemes will suggest themselves. This is the very first step from layout 'selection' (i.e. from existing designs) to layout 'planning' when you embark on the design of the layout that *you* want, within the parameters of the track that you have available.

Of course, knowing *what* you want is the difficult part at first, which is why the original experience with the train set as described above is so valuable. It is important eventually to break free from the rigidity of the standard straights and sharp radial curves of the set track. The use of flexible track is the way to do this, because it means that you are no longer restricted to fixed radii curves. The use of this type of track will be explained in the next chapter, but from the planning point of view it means that a greater degree of freedom has been achieved. Before we go on to explore this freedom, a few definitions will be useful at this stage to avoid the need for explanations later on.

'The six foot' or 'six foot way' is the area between pairs of main running lines which, in 00 (4mm to 1ft scale) can be derived by placing the track centres at $1\frac{3}{4}$in (4.5mm) apart. However, unless all your curves are likely to be at least 3ft 6in (107cm) it would be as well to keep to the recommended 2in (51mm) centre line to centre line. This is to avoid the possibility of passing trains coming into contact with each other due to the excessive end and centre swing of both locomotives and bogie coaches on the tight curves and the rocking from side to side of the model vehicles. In fact, for very tight curves, it might even be necessary to use $2\frac{1}{2}$in (64mm), but try and avoid such unrealistic curves. To get some idea of just how unrealistic our model curves are, consider that quite ordinary 2-6-0 and 4-6-0 British Standard steam locomotives were

quoted as being capable of traversing a *minimum* radius of 6 chains (1 chain = 22 yards = 66 feet = 792 inches (2011cm)) which in 00 at 1/76 = $10\frac{1}{2}$in (26.6cm)). So the equivalent curve quoted as a minimum in 00 would be $6 \times 10\frac{1}{2} = 63$in (160cm)!

Points and crossings

Points, or turn outs, are known as Left-Hand or Right-Hand, depending on which way they diverge from the straight, and as 'facing' or 'trailing' depending on the direction in which they are traversed by trains. Both facing and trailing 'cross-overs' are illustrated, each formed by a pair of points between adjacent lines. The facing points are R.H., while the trailing ones are L.H.;

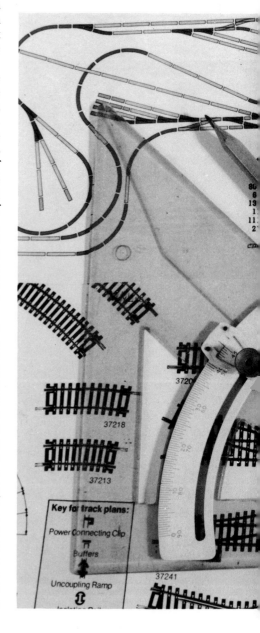

37200

37218

37213

Key for track plans:

Power Connecting Clip

Buffers

Uncoupling Ramp

37241

the arrows indicate the direction of travel. Generally, facing points are not used to lead straight off from a main line to any track formations such as sidings, goods sheds, locomotive depots that terminate in dead ends. This is to avoid the danger of a train being incorrectly diverted at speed into such areas, with disastrous results. Entry to all such areas is almost always by reversal over trailing points. Of course, facing points are required at junctions. This is illustrated by a double junction formed by Y-points, both arms at the points diverging away from one another.

Where one track crosses another, a diamond crossing is used. When a curve is superimposed on to a diamond crossing

connecting a pair of adjacent arms, it is known as a single 'slip-point' or 'single-slip'. The illustration shows its use to provide both a trailing crossover and a trailing connection into, say, a goods yard. Where both sides of the diamond are provided with curves, it becomes a 'double slip' widely used in areas of complex pointwork such as station throats and yards, but never on the open main line. So far the diagrams have been drawn showing both rails of the track, but this is not necessary when designing a layout and from now on a single line will be used to indicate a track. Point blades are indicated as open on the route requiring the point to be reversed and as a full line on the 'normal' position.

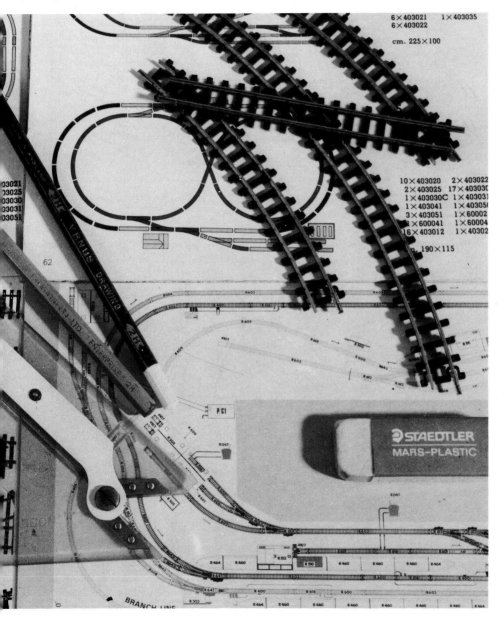

Preceding pages: When drawing up the final design of your layout, make use of commercially available radius curves to avoid creating too sharp a curve.

Left: Manufacturers' catalogues are a fruitful source of layout ideas and it is worth buying a selection.

Right: An advantage with a 'train set' is that various track layouts can be tried on a large table or baseboard by simply rearranging the plug-together track lengths, but a permanent layout should be the aim of every enthusiast where possible.

Opposite: Some of the basic pointwork with which the newcomer must become familiar. Nomenclature varies slightly from country to country, but principles are common. Doubling to cross other tracks makes things look complicated; start by considering whether the geometry indicates trailing or facing turnouts.

Below: Curves on model layouts generally have to be much sharper than in true scale, and one of the resulting effects is illustrated below. The throw of the locomotives and rolling stock requires that tracks are separated by an over-scale distance on tight bends.

Using space wisely

When planning a layout, the first consideration is the amount of space which is available. There have been many ingenious methods of utilising the available space which seems to be in such short supply

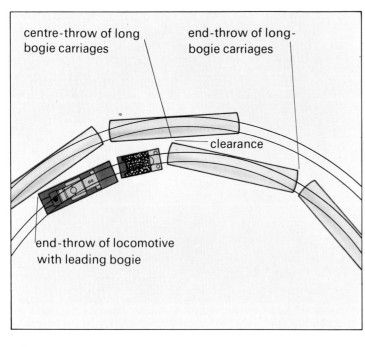

within the modern home. To some extent, the amount and shape of the available space will determine the basic concept of the layout.

If you are fortunate enough to have an entire spare room at your disposal, there is a strong likelihood that you will opt for an 'island' site in the middle of the room, giving access to the layout from all sides. This will mean that your layout will probably be on the 'oval' concept. However, give thought to the possibility of extending the layout out to the walls of the room, giving a longer 'route mileage', and give yourself access to the layout from the inside. A 'lift out', or hinged section, can be provided in the vicinity of the door, provided that it opens outwards: if the door opens inwards, either rehang the door or keep the layout well clear to avoid restricting its opening. The layout itself can still be continuous of course, which is a better way of describing 'based on the oval'.

People who are totally inexperienced in the model railway hobby sometimes believe that the track *must* be continuous, for the trains to run at all! This, of course, is not true and a layout can just as easily be non-continuous, as we shall see later, but

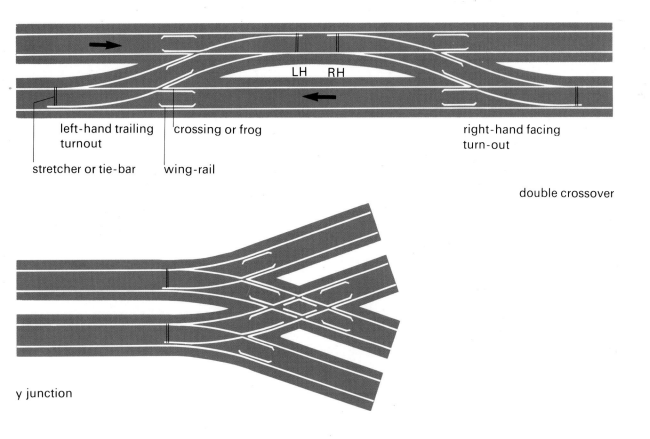

left-hand trailing
turnout

crossing or frog

right-hand facing
turn-out

stretcher or tie-bar

wing-rail

LH RH

double crossover

y junction

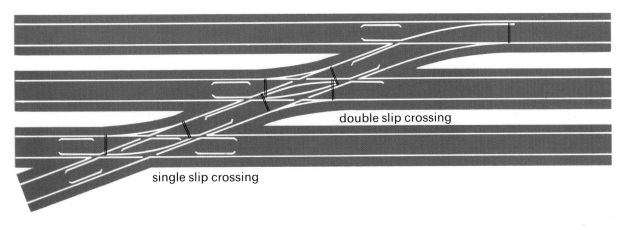

double slip crossing

single slip crossing

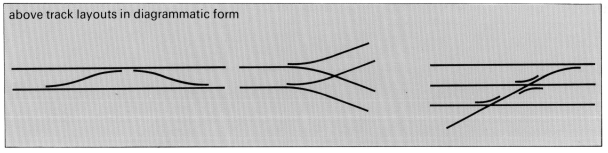

above track layouts in diagrammatic form

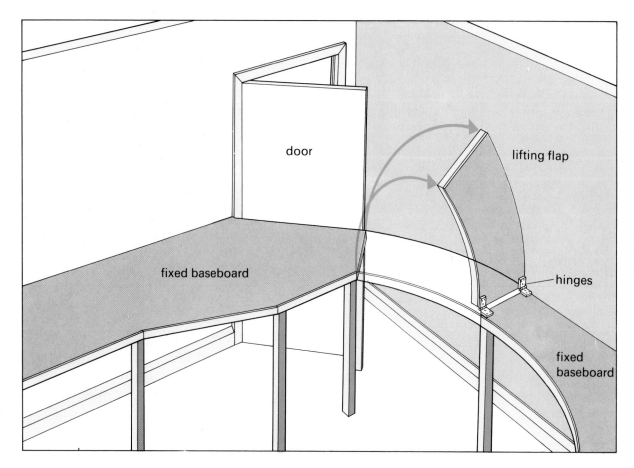

door

lifting flap

fixed baseboard

hinges

fixed baseboard

A layout run round the walls of a room requires provision for access, and a door positioned in a corner is always more difficult than one set in a straight wall. A flap is desirable even with an outward-opening door, to avoid the necessity of ducking under the track to crawl in.

first let us continue with our search for space. Garages have been used, often with the main part of the layout disposed across the end of the building with narrow, shelf-borne tracks along one or both sides. Do not, however, restrict the width of the garage so much that the car door cannot be opened! Faced with this problem, some layouts have been made which fold away along one wall, being extended for operation when the car is out of the garage.

Take a look at your loft area. A reasonable amount of space may be found amid the trusses and rafters, but a fair amount of preparation such as flooring, insulation, boarding in, lighting etc. will have to be done first. Insulation of the roof against the excessive heat of summer and the bitter cold of winter is very important. Nevertheless, some very snug railway rooms have been built in lofts and also in garden sheds where the problems of insulation and heating are much the same.

Finally, there is always the garden itself and some extensive layouts have been run from a garden shed or garage out into the garden and back. But garden railways are something of a special case and, whilst

receiving this passing mention, they will not be dealt with here.

Track formations

Having mentioned non-continuous layouts, let us now consider the different forms that layouts can take and then perhaps consider the further development of each. Look at the accompanying variations on the plain continuous formation—'A' being a 'figure of eight' and 'B' being a 'folded figure of eight'. Both can be flat, using a diamond crossing, but main lines crossing each other on the flat is not the sort of thing one would normally find on most real railways (although not entirely unknown in America). A bridge and gradients are introduced to avoid the other, not very prototypical, arrangements. In 4mm : 1ft scale, a clearance of about $2\frac{1}{2}$–3in (64–76mm) is required for the bridge, which in turn necessitates quite a long approach to keep the gradient to reasonable proportions, especially if it lies wholly or partially on a curve. The rolling resistance of a train is considerably increased under these conditions, restricting the length of trains that can be run. Naturally, if the layout is relatively small this state will apply anyway, but nevertheless allow not less than about 1 : 30 for the gradient and very much more if possible.

A completely different approach, however, is also shown: an end to end configuration. Trains move from one station to the other and back again. Simple in concept perhaps, but requiring a lot more additional facilities than one might suppose at first glance. For instance, you will need a means of getting the locomotive from one end of its train to the other and, unless it is a tank engine, a means of turning it. But bear in mind, these are real railway requirements, which means that the layout can only be properly planned and operated by meeting these requirements. This is of course the point where real railway modelling starts, the beginning of that absorbing interest of finding out what real railways are all about.

The two stations should be as far apart as possible, which means that the railway can be concentrated in two distinct areas, with the main lines between them traversing quite narrow shelving along one or more walls, leaving the majority of the room for its normal or intended use such as a bedroom. The fact that the two stations are apart also suggests that the running can now be shared between two operators, one at each end, sending and receiving trains. This latter facility may not be required, in which case the 'out and back' or boomerang layout may be more attractive. Trains departing from the terminus station will traverse the loop and return to the station. The locomotive will need to be released from its train, run round to the other end, turned, watered and coaled and put back on to its train, ready for another departure. Goods trains will need to be shunted and disposed of in the goods yard sidings. The loop can be curled back on itself to go behind, or even under, the terminus station to provide a longer run, and if pointwork is introduced, the 'out and back' becomes combined with the 'continuous run' type of layout. So any number of circuits can be completed before the points are changed to return the train to its destination. Furthermore, a locomotive driven over the three sides of the triangle will automatically be turned end on end, thus eliminating the need for a turntable; a very useful facility and one that has been used where appropriate on the prototype.

Finally, we introduce the concept of the

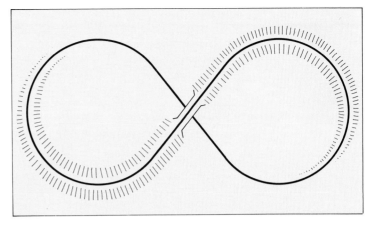

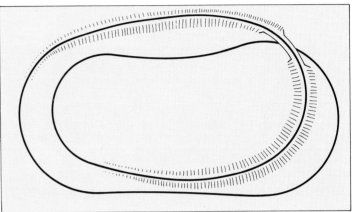

'hidden section', 'hidden sidings' or as it is nearly always called, 'the fiddle yard'. Essentially, this consists of a series of sidings which form a 'magazine' of made up trains any of which, by the setting of the appropriate route through the pointwork, can be brought into the station area, dealt with and subsequently despatched back into the empty siding off stage. Thus, the fiddle yard represents the ultimate destination of all trains leaving the terminus.

But, the station need not be a terminus. It can be a through station with a fiddle yard at each end which provides the capability of having non-stop express trains as part of the scene. Once again, bend the track to fit the available space. If it is continued far enough, it becomes logical to join up the two sets of sidings into one long fiddle yard and we have arrived back at the continuous layout. Trains, however, do not chase their tails, because a programme of trains can be operated as on an end to end, when each train passes once only through the station in either direction during an operating session, and yet a locomotive can be 'run in' by letting it go round and round as required.

The upper sketch is A a straightforward figure of eight, and the lower is B, a 'folded' figure of eight. Either could use a flat diamond crossing, but a bridge would be more realistic and gives the opportunity of introducing embankments or cuttings to add to scenic interest.

Aspects to consider

We are now moving towards more advanced modelling, because as one has seen, the operating pattern, the numbers, types and even lengths of trains are to be considered as part of the overall planning exercise. For instance, it is important that there is some sort of balance between the total accommodation within the hidden section and the facilities provided outside, on the visual model. It is no use providing 10-coach train lengths in the fiddle yard if the platform roads of your terminus can only accommodate 4-coach trains; you will not be able to run a 30 wagon freight train into a terminus goods yard with storage space for only 15 vehicles. Remember that the formation of track chosen largely determines the sort of layout that can be produced. For example, the small point-to-point or even hidden section-to-terminus format are less likely to be suitable for depicting main line operation. These are much more suited instead to a branch line or small suburban type of situation.

A layout need not necessarily contain a station area at all. A model of a locomotive depot can provide a most suitable background for a collector of locomotive models. An interesting operating pattern can be planned to include receiving and despatching locomotives 'on and off shed', with, in addition, all the ancillary movements involving loco coal and sand wagons, the disposal of the empty wagons and the removal of ash and sludge from the water softening plant. This would be quite a full and interesting programme with not a passenger coach in sight! But of course, if you do not know how things were done in M.P.D.s (Motive Power Depots) or loco yards you will have to find out—so again you can see that the building of model railways will require a fair amount of study and research. Fortunately there is no shortage of books and publications.

Another important aspect that should be borne in mind during the planning stages is the landscape through which your railway will run. Try and visualise and

Three basic layouts. The first is a simple, straight, end-to-end layout suitable for one wall, the second is an end-to-end layout along two walls. The alternative with limited space is an out-and-back loop, using a single station, which can be combined with pointwork and a continuous loop if desired.

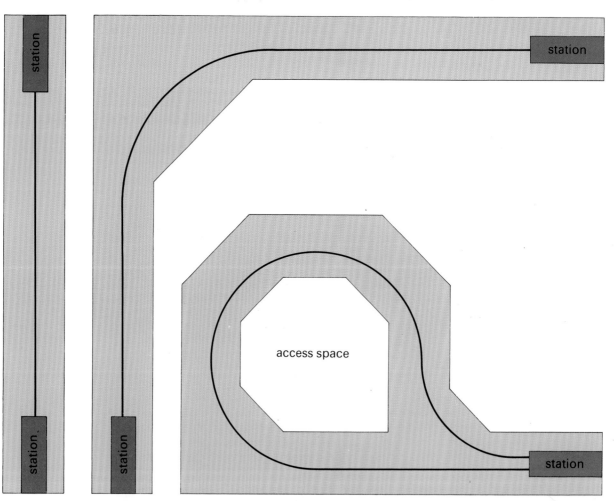

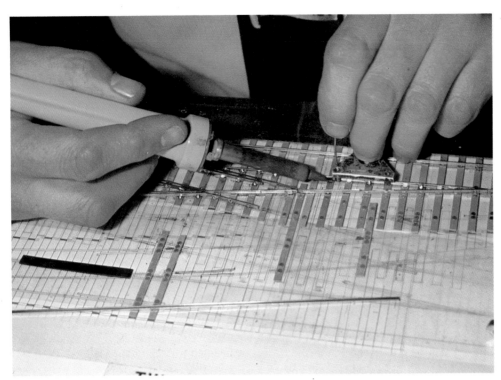

Making one's own points is not something to be recommended to every beginner, though with care and common sense it is not too difficult. Kits are available, and modern copper-clad laminate (printed circuit board) makes soldering a simple and straightforward operation.

Three more limited-space layouts, the first of which is for either a corner or island site, depending on ease of access. Note that it can be used for continuous running if required. The others are variations on end-to-end layouts, using hidden sidings instead of a second station.

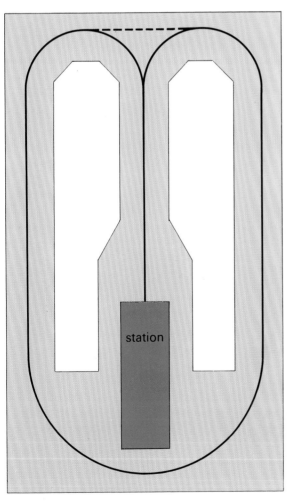

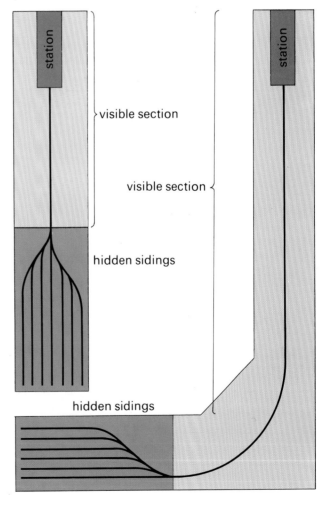

make provision for landscape features at the same time that the track formation is being worked out. Remember too, that railways are often elevated above the level of the surrounding countryside as well as being level with or below it. The next chapter will deal with the baseboard aspects, but it can be seen that side views, or even sections of the proposed layout, are just as important as plan views.

To begin with it is necessary to draw a plan of the layout in order to see exactly how we want it to be. We can then correct and alter points or even change our mind and start again if necessary! It is far better to work it all out beforehand so that you will avoid time-consuming and even expensive alterations to your layout. Possible damage may be caused by lifting track and pointwork after the layout has been built.

Ideas can be sketched quite quickly freehand, but do not be tempted to proceed with construction on the basis of sketches alone, however elaborate and detailed. Such sketches have a habit of turning out to be too big for the available space, chiefly because pointwork occupies much more space than it would seem. It is possible to expand the marking out at the full size stage to take advantage of the last inch or two of space, but it is not easy to condense, however. This usually results in reducing the radii of curves to include it all, which is not an ideal solution to a problem. It is, therefore, important to know the dimen-

sions of the particular track that you are contemplating using. One well known manufacturer of model railway equipment (Peco) supplies planning cut-outs of pointwork to enable the sorting out of ideas and trial formations to be undertaken quickly and reasonably accurately, but it is still a good idea finally to translate the scheme into a drawing. The layout is not going to be built in five minutes, and that drawing is going to be needed for reference until all the track is laid. Some modellers even go to the trouble of building a scale model of a layout before starting!

Never cut clearances to the absolute minimum on the drawing (from the edge of the board for instance). Remember that it is to a reduced scale and so any slight errors will be magnified when marking out full size. If you have not got access to a drawing board with parallel motion ruler or T square, it is a good idea to use squared (graph) paper, adopting a scale to suit the particular paper. There is no need to draw the track as two rails, always draw centre lines. It is the position of the track centres which you will be marking out on the baseboards for positioning the track.

Long, shallow flowing curves are more attractive and more typical of the prototype than a series of short straights and small radius curves. Curves can be made to change their amount of curvature by using more than one centre for their construction. Set yourself a minimum radius. This self-

A simple loop layout can be vastly improved by concealing a section of track beneath scenery and incorporating a fiddle-yard. Ideally access should be possible to the back of the concealed section. The second illustration shows how curves can be blended in using circles of different radii.

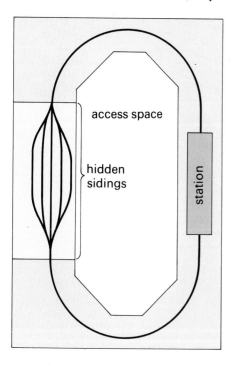

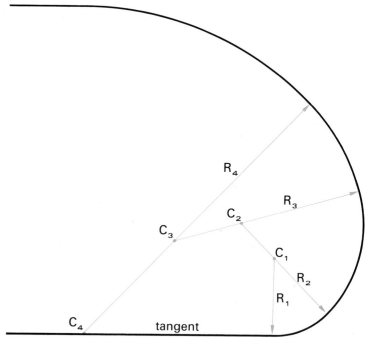

imposed restriction will pay dividends both in the ultimate appearance and running qualities of the finished layout. Try drawing a layout with nothing less than 3ft (91cm) radii and see how you get on within your allotted space. You may have to reduce this, but do so as little as you can, away from the main line if possible. Where curves have to be tight, try to restrict their use to where they can be effectively hidden or disguised, either in cuttings or beyond a tunnel mouth; try to design them away from the main viewing area.

Another aspect to think of in the planning stage is access. For example, the corner of a layout may be formed by the corner of a room and tracks for a goods yard might be sited in that corner because it looks like a useful space on your drawing. Remember that it may be necessary to provide an access flap in the base board to enable the tracks to be laid initially and to be reached subsequently for cleaning and even to re-rail vehicles that have become derailed. Measure the distance which you can comfortably reach over a table and include arcs of this dimension on your layout drawing where access looks doubtful.

When designing your own track formations without reference to particular situations on the prototype, there is a tendency to avoid possible operating snags. For example a point can be designed to enable a locomotive to run from say A to D without having to make three reversals of direction and using other points. It is included on the drawing forgetting two very important aspects. First, on the real railway there were very often many instances when going from 'A' to 'D' was anything but straightforward; secondly, and even more importantly, you are going to build the layout to have the fun of operating it. So why design all the operating fun out of it? Another example of this is when a release crossover at the buffer stop end of a terminus platform is often provided to enable the locomotive to 'escape' from that end of the train and proceed as previously described. If, however, no release crossover is provided, and this was not unknown, then a station pilot engine will have to be called into use to transfer the empty coaches from the arrival platform either into carriage sidings or direct into the departure platform, thereby releasing the train locomotive. Additional operating interest is thus imparted to the layout and also saving the cost of the installation of a couple of turnouts!

Often the first layout to be designed by a modeller in the initial wave of enthusiasm is later remembered with something of horror! One may begin by having only the vaguest idea what was involved in building and operating a layout, coupled with an ambitious vision and only the haziest practical knowledge of the workings of real railways.

Spend some time reading the hobby magazines to see what advice they offer on the subject. Each issue usually carries one or more descriptive articles about layouts together with photographs and a drawing. There are also contributions from dedicated modellers, trade reviews and so on. Bound volumes of back numbers, providing hours of interesting and instructive research, can be requested and obtained from public libraries. This approach is to be recommended, as the more reading that is done with regard to the hobby, the more it becomes absorbed. It is a good idea to study books on prototype which will help you to get as close as possible to the real thing.

A practical exercise

Sufficient guidelines have now been given to help you with your planning, but there is nothing like experience for making the pitfalls clear. So try planning layouts as exercises, without any real thought of building any of them. You may find that one of your planning doodles might suddenly become the inspiration for just the layout you were looking for. Before we leave the design aspect let us follow a brief exercise and go through the various steps required to achieve a layout design as a practical example. The graph paper we have obtained is to some peculiar standard that defies precise definition, but do not let us worry about that. We will designate each small square as 1in (Imperial measure will be used throughout this example but 1cm per square would be a suitable choice for metric measure). Let us assume that we have at our disposal an area within 10 × 6ft (120 × 72in). We shall also decide that we want a terminus to a hidden section. Tentatively, let us define the baseboard areas: say 2ft wide in the form of an L, allowing two boards for the 6ft dimension and two for the remaining 8ft dimension. For the time being we will assume that the pairs of boards are equal in length (i.e. two at 3ft and two at 4ft) as this will be advan-

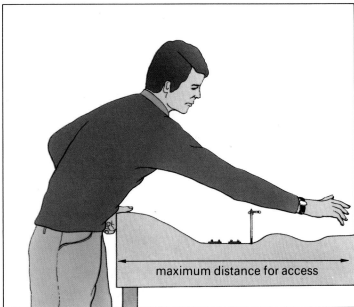

tageous for storage and/or transport. The station area will have to be along the long leg of the L as it will be too cramped to be squeezed in the other leg. Position the main line 6in from the baseboard edge and then strike a 3ft radius to turn it through 90° on to the hidden section board. This leaves a nice area in the top LH corner which will probably be just right for a goods yard.

With regard to the station, we want to run 4-coach trains, so, allowing about 10in for a coach and 9in for a tender 0-6-0 or 2-6-0 locomotive, we can mark in the desired length of the main platform, making it 3in wide which represents about 19ft in 4mm : 1ft scale. Reasonable so far, but possible problems in that hidden section area. There is only 29in of straight after the curve, and there is no pointwork as yet to form the ladder of sidings which we require, and which will occupy a fair amount of space. We can try placing a point, positioned on the curve and just on the corner board, strike a tangent to the curve and then blend in to meet a siding at 2in from the outside edge. Now, pitch off our 10in lengths for coaches (only four, but without a locomotive) and that would foul any additional points which will be required for any further sidings which we try to add. This design appears to be a non-starter.

So, we shall try a 30in radius striking from the main line position as before. There is no point in working on the station area until we have solved this hidden section problem. A few sidings at 2in centres are

When designing a layout, keeping things within comfortable reach is easy to overlook. Measure your reach at the appropriate height beforehand, and remember that replacing a derailed vehicle on the track is quite difficult if it can only just be reached.

Opposite: Complex trackwork at the approach to a station on a German H0 layout. When tracks diverge, width naturally increases, bringing potential problems of reaching over them. Extensive trackwork in a large goods yard is best with access from both sides rather than against a wall.

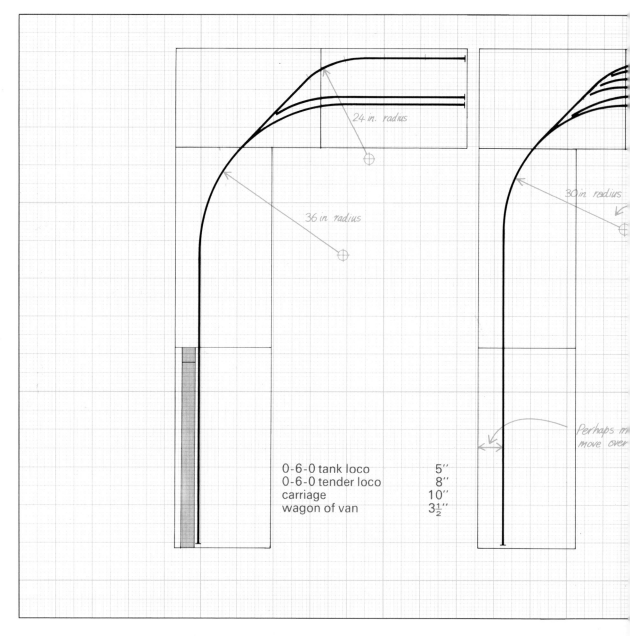

24 in. radius

36 in radius

30 in radius

Perhaps m
move over

0-6-0 tank loco	5″
0-6-0 tender loco	8″
carriage	10″
wagon of van	3½″

positioned, but by applying our measure of 10in per coach, it can be seen that even on the longest one there is only going to be room for three. Perhaps we ought to settle for three, which will be a pity, but there seems to be nothing else for it. However, what if we come round the other side of the available space for our fiddle yard? Will there be enough room between? Yes, we find we can swing a 30½in radius right round and construct a ladder of six sidings, making the longest one meet our requirement of 4 × 10in coaches and 1 × 8in locomotive. The six sidings will fit on to a board 12in wide (say 13in to be safe at this stage) so there is plenty of access space. A

joint line at 3ft 6in is clear of all pointwork, so these two boards can also be a 'pair'. The main line in the station area has in fact been moved a little nearer to the centre of the board, as it has been recognised that a little more space beyond the platform will be required. For instance, it will make it a little more interesting if we have a bay platform, and beyond that a reception road for the goods trains which will be operating to and from the terminus goods yard. This, in the form of additional siding accommodation, is now added to the reception road, which also serves as a head shunt for the yard.

A run-round-loop is next added to the

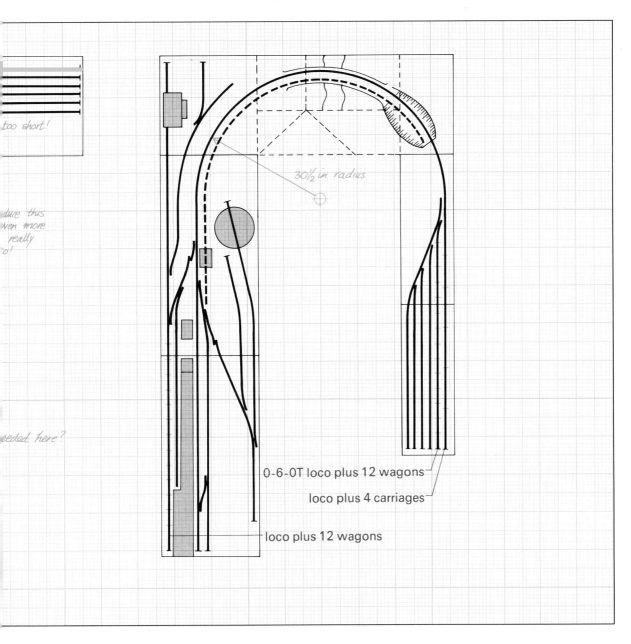

too short!

duce this
en more
really
o!

30½ in radius.

eeded here?

0-6-0T loco plus 12 wagons

loco plus 4 carriages

loco plus 12 wagons

main platform road to allow the loco-motives of arriving trains to get clear of the coaches and proceed into the locomotive yard, which is the next facility to be added in the available space on the inside of the station area. This has now been shown with a turn-table, but that might be ex-changed for a small engine shed. With a goods shed, a signal box, and a coaling stage added, we have now got a workable layout.

The light and heavy dashed lines show alternative baseboard arrangements that now become a possibility once the main line curve has been decided upon. There is also a hint of a double-track main line. It is worth looking at the implications if this is thought to be a future development. Can the way be provided now, in order to avoid too much rebuilding at a later stage? For instance, if we incorporate a viaduct or bridge over a river then shall we make it wide enough to take that second track later? There are many examples of this having happened on real railways, so it will not be inaccurate even if it is never doubled. Note that the idea of the viaduct now requires that side view discussed earlier. As you can see, the design appears to evolve. This example is still not perfect, but suffi-ciently developed to illustrate the stages and thought processes that are involved.

Stages in planning a layout, as described in the text. First draughts should be made on graph paper, which simplifies accurate scaling. For full-scale marking out, a lath drilled for a pencil and pivoting on a sharp nail enables large radius circles to be drawn.

TRACK CONSTRUCTION

Having now planned your layout, you are keen to build it and start running trains. There are still a few more steps to take before that day arrives. For instance, you will need to plan where to site it. Presumably you are not thinking of spreading it out over the lounge carpet; you are much more likely to be thinking in terms of a table top, probably a standard 8×4ft (240×120cm) sheet of hardboard, braced with a light framework, on which you will fix by some means, not yet determined, your projected railway. If, however, these were your first ideas, then you should think again. A baseboard built on these lines would be unwieldy, unstable, noisy and almost unreachable over part of its area, especially if located in a corner of a room. Do not think of a fixed area such as 8×4ft (240×120cm) into which as much railway as possible is to be fitted, but think first of the railway and then work out the support required. For example, a long, thin end-to-end layout can be accommodated on a relatively narrow shelf fixed to the wall of the room with commercial brackets. Such a shelf, leading perhaps to a wider board on a window sill or bay window area for a station complex, could make an ideal permanent layout in a bedroom, without totally compromising the normal use of the room. Even a spare room may be needed occasionally!

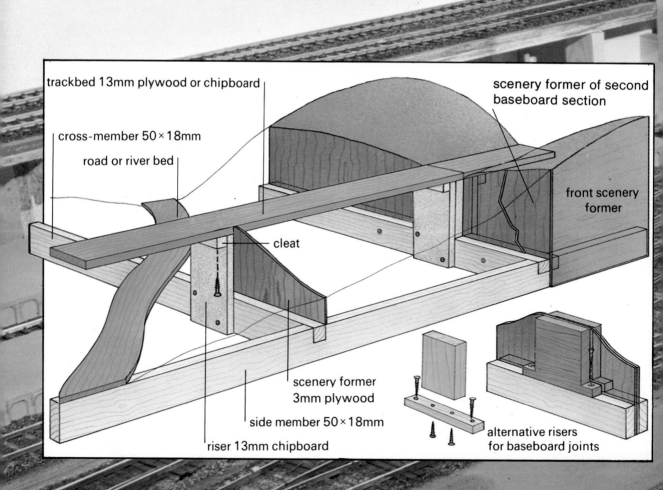

trackbed 13mm plywood or chipboard

scenery former of second baseboard section

cross-member 50×18mm

road or river bed

front scenery former

cleat

scenery former 3mm plywood

side member 50×18mm

riser 13mm chipboard

alternative risers for baseboard joints

Preceding pages: The photograph shows part of a German 0 gauge layout by Rolf Ertmer under construction. Composition board, 8mm thick, forms the baseboard, reinforced by an additional strip of 8mm board beneath the tracks themselves. The inset shows a typical section of scenery framework. Separating sections obviously need matching formers; it is best to construct the scenic base with the sections assembled, cutting through as work proceeds, in order to ensure smooth joints on the surface.

Construction

It is important that a railway baseboard must be firm and rigid to resist sagging and warping. A lot of time and effort is going to be expended on the layout itself, and what a waste and disappointment it will be if the baseboards, the foundations if you like, are skimped and prove inadequate. On the other hand, avoid building a structure of such a size or complexity that the only way of moving it is to dismantle it completely. Even if you never intend to take it to exhibitions, you might, one day, need to move house! Anything longer than about six feet should be built as readily separated units or modules. In fact, a layout that is intended for exhibition work might well comprise a number of units 4ft long × 1 or 2ft wide (120 × 30 or 60cm), making them readily transportable by car (hatchbacks or estate cars at least).

The basic framework should be $\frac{3}{4}$in or 1in × 2in (18mm or 25mm × 51mm) planed timber members, cross braced with members of the same section at about 1ft (30cm) intervals. Butt joints can be used, but it is advisable to reinforce them (at least at the corners) with plywood gussets. Of course, half laps are better. All joints should be screwed and glued. Drill all screw holes the appropriate size in each member, to avoid too much hard work in driving the screws, and also avoid the risk of splitting the wood. Before fixing any top, provide cut-outs in *all* internal members to facilitate wiring at a later stage.

With modules which are to be separated after track has been laid, it is vital that a means of accurately re-locating them is provided. Three possible methods are illustrated: at A bolts and wing nuts serve the dual purpose of locating and fixing. This requires that the holes are a close, tight fit on the bolts, which must be square to the interface and parallel to each other. The holes are reinforced with metal plates, otherwise in time the holes will enlarge and the accurate location lost, leading to stepped rails at the joint and consequent derailments. A more satisfactory method, shown at B, is to use a pattern makers' dowel to obtain, and keep, the accuracy of

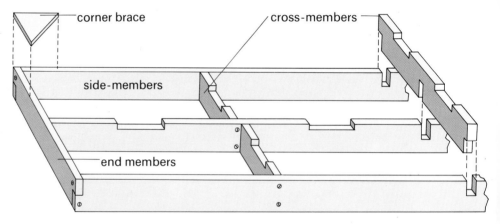

corner brace — cross-members — side-members — end members

A firm and rigid (but not too heavy) base is essential. Jointed parts are best if your carpentry is reasonable, but butt-jointed cross-members can be staggered to allow screwing in place while the glue is wet. Methods of positively jointing sectional layouts are shown below.

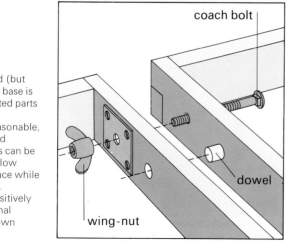

coach bolt — dowel — wing-nut

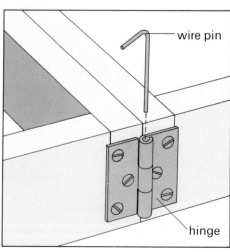

wire pin — hinge

location and relegate the role of the bolt or bolts to fixing only, in which case the hole can be of adequate clearance, making dismantling and assembly so much easier. Ideally, adjacent end members should be prepared as a pair when fitting the dowels and drilling for bolts, each then being built into its module. The drilling must be done truly normal to the joint and parallel one to the other, otherwise the dowels will lock in the socket and prevent separation. A pillar drill, or a drilling block which itself has been accurately prepared, must be used. Finally, at C is shown a method using 'flap-back' hinges. The two modules are clamped together, the top surfaces being flush one with the other, and then at each side the hinge is attached across the joint. When fixed, the hinge pins are driven out and replaced by a longer, angled pin as shown. Withdrawal of the pins enables the boards to be separated and accurate replacement is determined by the mating of the hinges again. Use a square to ensure they are positioned truly vertically, otherwise locking up can occur.

L-Girder construction

In the USA there is a somewhat different approach to layout or railroad pike building. Preference is given to static, permanent structure and in this context the L-Girder construction system has a lot to commend it. Instead of individual boards and rectangular, regular bracing, the main support consists of two inverted L-shaped timber beams along the full length of the site. Perhaps no more than four legs (two per beam) are used. Joists are secured by screws from underneath the top flange of the L-beams, spanning the gap between and extending the layout in both cases as far as it is required. No joints are required, joists are put precisely where they are needed, not even at right angles to the beams, but wherever a riser is required to support the track bed, which is attached, again by screws from underneath, through cleats attached at the top of the risers. Modifications are easy, as joints can be unscrewed and moved about, or additional joists added at will. It is a very versatile system, but not suitable for portable structures.

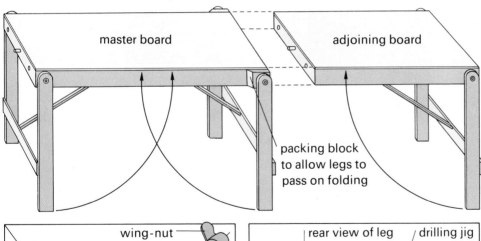

master board   adjoining board

packing block
to allow legs to
pass on folding

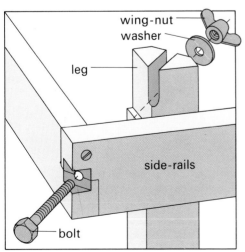

wing-nut
washer

leg

side-rails

bolt

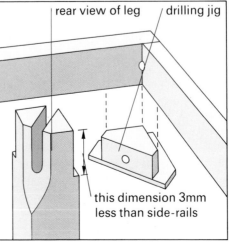

rear view of leg   drilling jig

this dimension 3mm
less than side-rails

Portable or semi-portable layouts need folding or, better, removable legs. A lean-to section is shown in the upper drawing, together with a method of spacing legs to fold flush on the main section. Adjustable-height bolt-on legs are illustrated in the lower drawing.

Supporting the layout

Assuming that the layout will not be placed on the floor, then the boards will require some form of support. A small, single-board layout may be accommodated on an existing piece of furniture, but generally it is better to provide the layout with its own legs. Trestles are sometimes suggested, but on the whole these require more timber and carpentry than individual legs and are thus more expensive in material and time. The actual height of the layout is largely a matter of personal preference. For instance, a height of 4ft 6in or even 5ft (135–150cm) gives a more realistic viewpoint to the individual, but is too high for an exhibition. An average height seems to lie between 3ft and 3ft 6in (91–107cm). The trestle table method of providing support is shown. Because of the internal cross-bracing, the legs have to be arranged to fold on the outside, or lie entirely below the framework, increasing the stored height of each unit. Also, with the legs permanently attached, the handling weight of each module is increased. Furthermore, any facility for adjustment to accommodate uneven floors is yet another addition to the scheme. One point that is illustrated is the fact that only one board, the master board, requires four legs. The remainder, as a lean-to, needs just two. Also illustrated is a specially-designed method of support. The legs, fashioned from 2×2in (50×50mm) timber, the tops being cut as shown, are attached to or dismantled from the boards by sliding on to or off the bolts by means of the diagonal slot, cut to suit the bolt size being used (possibly $\frac{3}{8}$in or 9mm). The wing nut can be tightened or slackened off accordingly. A small drill jig, as shown, is used to drill all four corners of all boards. The legs, being universal, can be fitted to any board, and so any of them can become a 'master', a useful facility when working on one board at a time. It has been found that no other bracing is required. Normally the rails of the boards rest on the $\frac{1}{4}$in (6mm) ledges, but if unevenness in the floor has to be accommodated, a leg can be tightened up whilst not yet 'bottomed'. An alternative is, of course, to fit screwed adjusters as sold in DIY shops for light table legs.

The trackbed

For a flat topped board, wood fibre insulation board is often recommended, largely because it will take and hold track pins without pre-drilling. As the pinning-down of track is not recommended here, using wood-fibre board, apart from its sound-deadening qualities, has no real benefit. Chipboard $\frac{1}{2}$in (12mm) thick or $\frac{1}{2}$ or $\frac{3}{8}$in

Separating sections of layout require extreme accuracy and rigidity in order that on reassembly the tracks line up absolutely spot-on. A joint on a straight length is to be preferred, but methods of dealing with less convenient joints and the wiring associated with them are illustrated later.

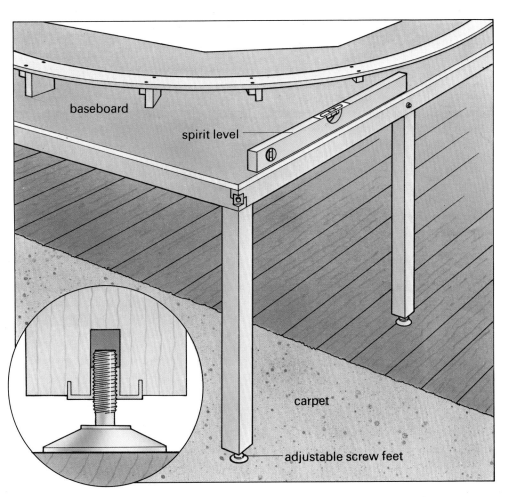

baseboard

spirit level

carpet

adjustable screw feet

A level baseboard is desirable as, apart from unsteadiness, trains may be running slightly uphill in one direction and downhill in the other. Inexpensive screwed feet may be used in place of, or together with, legs slotted and bolted as shown on page 37. Even a carpet causes a considerable tilt.

(12 or 9mm) ply can be used. Drill and glue the board and screw it to the framework, countersinking the screw heads. (With chipboard or ply the cross-bracing pitch may be safely increased up to 2ft 6in (76cm) without danger of hogs and sags.)

For open-top construction, however, ply or chipboard are essential. The baseboards can be covered with sheets cut to suit, the track formation marked out and then the portions carrying track cut out along each edge using a power jigsaw. However, this is extremely wasteful of material, effectively cancelling out the cost-effectiveness of the open board method. Instead, marking-out can be done on sheets of cardboard or thick paper, which are cut out to make templates. These can then be nested together on to the ply or chipboard to ensure the most economical use of the sheet. The sections of track bed so obtained can now be positioned on the framework, carefully aligned, and each edge marked down where it crosses any frame member. Risers, to the height required, can now be prepared for each location, using off-cuts

of ply or any other suitable timber. You will need to attach a cleat of square or near-square stripwood using glue and screws at the top which should be pre-drilled to accept screws up into the track-bed. Fix the end risers, where the trackbed crosses joints, first. These must obviously be in pairs, one on each board. Then, using a straightedge or spirit level, push each ready-glued riser in turn up to the trackbed. Clamp each one in place, drill into the bracing member, screw it up and finally screw to the trackbed. By following this method you will then have a trackbed without humps.

An alternative to a cut-out trackbed utilises $\frac{1}{8}$in (3mm) ply cut into strips $\frac{1}{2}$in (12mm) wide. These strips, when laid on edge, can be formed in to any desired sequence of curves. Successive strips bonded together with glue built up into the required width of the trackbed. Whilst this method is extremely economical as regards plywood, it requires a great deal of glue. However, it is mentioned to illustrate the point that there are a number of ways of approaching any problem and it is a good idea to experiment with different solutions.

Marking out curves

Although the very first exercise in lay-out design and building will probably be carried out using the fixed geometry track that comes with a boxed train set, it can be expected that the restriction of fixed radii and rigid straight lengths of track will eventually give way to more ambitious designs. Possibly the existing layout will be extended using commercial flexible track, which can be bent to the desired curvature. This will give a freedom of design not possible with the set-tracks and the shallow, sweeping curves of the prototype can then be simulated.

In this connection, it will be as well to mention the problem of marking out large radius curves. You have already read about trammels (large beam compasses), but these are only really suitable for large scale work. Templates are also advocated, and commercially-produced radius templates are available. However, by far the best way of marking out a curve that joins up two spatially separate lines at an angle other than 180° is to use a *spline*, a long piece of square ($\frac{1}{4} \times \frac{1}{4}$in or 6×6mm) or rect-angular wood ($\frac{1}{8} \times \frac{1}{4}$ or $\frac{3}{8}$in, 3×6 or 9mm) or Perspex (Plexiglas) which can be

flexed between them. If it is held in place by suitable weights, a smooth, blending curve can be drawn on a natural transition from one straight to the other. A minimum-radius curve template will ensure that the spline is not flexed on a tighter curve than the minimum radius which you have set for your layout.

Points and trackwork

Pointwork, i.e. turn-outs and crossings (switches and diamonds or crossovers) require a wide range of choice for realistic formations. Some manufacturers have a wider range than others, so a careful study of catalogues and advice from experienced enthusiasts can help. Trackwork from different manufacturers are often com-pletely compatible, but it is advisable to keep to a single source to begin with. Commercial scale track, usually of soldered construction using printed circuit board sleepers (or ties) is also available. Often, however, the accompanying pointwork takes the form of construction kits, which if purchased already assembled are some-what expensive.

You can make your own trackwork, either soldering rail to printed circuit board (copper-clad) sleepers, or to ply-wood sleepers into which flatheaded rivets have been inserted to simulate the chairs of

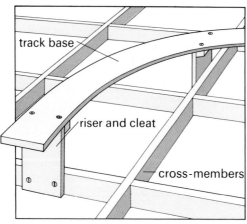

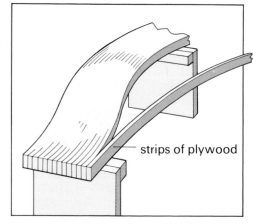

Rising or falling track bases can be cut from thick ply or similar material and supported by risers as drawn. A less common alternative is to use vertical laminations of ply strips. Marking out the curves on the ply or the baseboard is simplified by using a spline to achieve smooth transitions.

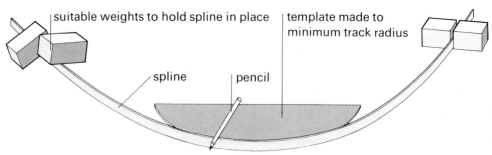

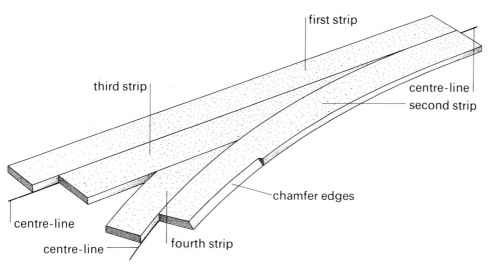

first strip

third strip

centre-line

second strip

centre-line

chamfer edges

centre-line

fourth strip

Strips of rubberised cork are recommended as the best underlay. Building up a turnout is illustrated; the joint lines between strips provide a guide for laying the actual track. The basic shape of the ballast is represented by chamfering off the edges at 45° with a sharp modelling knife.

the real track. Plain track is relatively easy to make, but pointwork does require the careful application of acquired skills, so it is not proposed to go into detail on the subject here. Much information can be readily obtained from the specialist magazines and national societies.

The chapter on Designing the Layout stressed the importance of making a scale drawing of the trackplan, and a full-sized plan must now be transferred on to the baseboard. In the case of open-top boards this will have been done already. The necessary pointwork, having been determined and acquired, can be used as templates to assist in the detail marking. Concentrate on getting the alignment of the pointwork correct so that it can be positioned without having to strain it to fit.

Fixing underlay

There are various reasons for the use of underlay, ranging from sound proofing to 'floating track' purposes. In essence it is there to simulate the depth of ballast that exists in the real formation. Foam underlays give rise to all sorts of track stability problems and are not recommended here. A flat, stable but flexible material is required and rubberised cork in strips (available at model shops), has been found to possess these desirable qualities, with an additional bonus. One inch (25mm) strips, glued either side of the marked centre line (using an impact adhesive which enables the strips to be tailored to the required curves whilst still remaining flat) will automatically reproduce the centre line as the joint line between the two strips. Therefore, no further marking out is necessary even after all the underlay is down. Four × 1in

(25mm) strips laid side by side will give track centres at 2in (50mm) pitch which is a B.R.M.S.B. recommended dimension. All junctions occasioned by turn-outs and crossings can be dealt with quite easily. The outside edges are chamfered off at about 45° using a sharp craft knife.

Track-laying

Track-laying can now begin. Start with the point formations. Position them as indicated by the centre line on the underlay and lightly fix down to the underlay using track pins driven home, or a small office stapling machine can be used just to hold the sleepers in place. Cut portions of flexible track to join up turn-outs and crossings accurately using a razor saw in conjunction with a small block of wood with two slots at rail gauge distance apart which can be pressed down over the track. This holds it firmly and provides a guide for the saw. Any burrs remaining can be removed with a small file. The rail fixing at the end sleeper will probably have to be cut away with a sharp knife to facilitate the insertion of a 'fish-plate' type rail joiner. These are a commercial product, usually supplied by the manufacturers of the track

Make a rail cutting guide by sawing two slots in a block of wood at accurate rail gauge distance and dead square to the reference face. The block will then hold the rails firmly and the reference face will guide a razor saw, enabling a precise match to be made with the next length of rail.

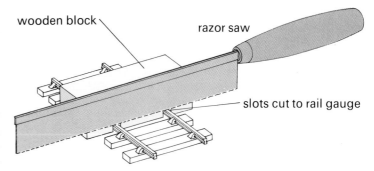

wooden block

razor saw

slots cut to rail gauge

in the form of a U sleeve, shaped to fit the bottom flange profile of the rail and so ensure alignment of rails one with the other. They should not be relied on for electrical continuity, although initially they will probably provide it. Also they should not be soldered to the rails as this might give rise to the problem of expansion, causing buckled track.

It will be at this stage that you must frequently obtain rail-level views along the running surfaces. You will be amazed to find kinks that are not at all apparent with normal viewing. Dog-legs at rail joints on curves must be watched for and eliminated as the work proceeds.

When a fair amount of the formation has been prepared in this way, mark the positions of all the point blade stretches (tie bars), remove the pins or staples and carefully lift the assembled trackage aside. Mask the marked areas to keep them free from glue. Spread the area with white P.V.A. glue, or one of the commercial lino tile cements. Remove the masks and re-position the trackwork, carefully aligning with track or tracks already laid.

Applying ballast

When you are satisfied that the track is down satisfactorily, cover the area with ballast, either granulated cork or granite chippings. Gently tamp down between the sleepers and over the chamfer of the under-lay. Place weights on the track to prevent it being moved inadvertently and leave it for the glue to set. The surplus ballast can then be brushed or tipped off for re-use. Note that pinning-down has not been referred to. If this is not done carefully, it can tend to 'quilt' the track. If pins are used, make sure that they are a sliding fit in the holes, and do not drive the pins hard home, but leave the head just proud of the sleeper. The object of pinning is not to hold down the track, but to prevent lateral movement until the glue sets.

An alternative method, which has much to commend it, is to leave the application of the ballast until after all the track is down, all electrical feed connections soldered on and test running has estab-lished that all is well. Only then is the dry ballast applied, being carefully brushed in place to lie between the sleepers and up the shoulders of the underlay. A light spraying with water to which has been added just a drop or two of liquid detergent (washing-up liquid) will help to break down surface

Opposite: The tunnel entrance on Rolf Ertmer's H0 'Repa-bahn II' layout leads to a spiral with five circles superimposed to produce quite a dramatic change of height. Since traffic on the layout is predominantly handled by steam locomotives, smoke traces on the tunnel portal are apposite.

tension, so that when a 50/50 dilution of white P.V.A. adhesive and water is applied with an eye dropper along the edges, it is rapidly soaked up by the damp ballast. Once the glue has set, the ballast will be found to be firmly and solidly held. Protect point blade stretches by inserting grease-proof paper or aluminium cooking foil which can be removed later when the glue has set.

Dealing with baseboard joints

At baseboard joints the track should be laid across the joint with the two boards firmly bolted together. Small brass screws, on either side of the joint and under each rail, can be adjusted by screwing in or out until the heads just touch the bottom of the rail. When the track is finally and firmly placed, the rails should be soldered to the screws and only then cut by means of a razor saw, across the joint.

It is important that the track does not cross a joint at too acute an angle. This will involve cutting across sleepers. If such a lie of the track cannot be avoided, there are two solutions. One is to provide a local tongue or projection in the baseboard top to fit into an identical rebate in the adjacent top. Of course with open-top boards the track bed on its raised substructure can be

jointed at a different angle to that of the main board structure.

The alternative is to have a short, removable portion of track which bridges the joint, attached to the track on either side by rail joiners which can be slid back to release the insert. This requires that rail fixings must be cut from two sleepers to provide the necessary clearance for the movement of the joiners. The main difficulty with this method concerns ballasting in the vicinity of the removable section. Loose ballast seems to be the only possibility, and then only when the layout is moved at very infrequent intervals.

Preparing for wiring

Although wiring has not yet been dealt with, at least one aspect must be considered at the track-laying stage. For the purposes of providing electrical isolation in certain circumstances, gaps in the rails have to be provided at certain specific places. With the circuits already determined, gaps cannot just be left in the course of laying, but need to be insulated with plastic rail joiners in lieu of the normal metal ones. In plain track it is easy enough to cut an isolating gap after the track is fixed down. It is a good idea to fill the gap with epoxy glue. This ensures that the gap is not bridged by

Irrespective of the angle of joint where a section of portable track separates, the rails themselves should always be cut square. Electrical continuity is assured by soldering wire bonds to the rail ends and connecting these beneath the baseboard, either as part of a multi-pin plug loom or with a separate plug.

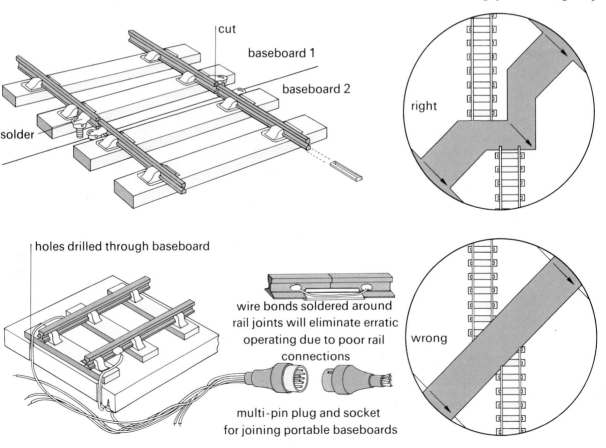

cut

baseboard 1

baseboard 2

solder

holes drilled through baseboard

wire bonds soldered around
rail joints will eliminate erratic
operating due to poor rail
connections

multi-pin plug and socket
for joining portable baseboards

right

wrong

expansion of the rails at a later date. However, gaps are seldom where one can get at them with a saw, since adjacent rails, especially in the crowded areas of pointwork, severely restrict the movement that can be applied to the saw.

Achieving realistic track

Finally, the one item that perhaps has the biggest impact in the achievement of realism is paint. Take a look at your nearest railway. Rails do not have a shiny metallic finish, apart from the well used running

An underside view of a joint in a portable layout. Blocks should be provided so that all wiring looms can be securely anchored.

Previous pages: This photograph encompasses most of the 'Repa-bahn II' H0 layout, with Altenbeken station in the centre.

Above: A large 0 gauge layout under construction by Rolf Ertmer—note the track plan in front of the controller's chair. The spiral of track was later concealed beneath scenic detail.

Opposite: Working the super-elevation into a curved track bed. It is incorrect—and looks it—simply to tilt the whole track bed, since in full-size the inner rail of each track is at the same height.

surface, and even this is fairly dull if a train hasn't traversed it for some considerable time. The sleepers (ties) are not a glossy black or even a glossy brown! The ballast is never a uniform grey colour (unless newly laid). Spray the whole of the track area with a thin, dirty brown paint (brush washings are usually ideal) and go over the sides of the rails with rust brown paint, but wipe the top of the rails clear of paint before it dries. Areas where locomotives normally stand for extended periods, such as water columns, at the end of station platforms and in motive power depots, should be made even darker to represent the dropped oil and ash. Attention to such detail will help enormously towards achieving overall realism.

Superelevation

This is the banking or 'cant' applied to the track at curves. When using table-top boards, the only way to achieve this in model form is to pack under the outer rail with taper packings. This is a difficult operation which only results in poor running and the modeller is advised to avoid this method. However, when using open-top boards, the track bed can be twisted when it takes up a natural transition. Intermediate risers, with squared tops, can be positioned up to the underside of the track-bed between the last horizontal top riser, and one of the required angles of 'twist'. The varying angle at each position is that of the riser itself relative to the framework or joists. Double track can be dealt with by cutting along between the tracks with a power jig saw, each separated portion being twisted, the inside one packed with local, parallel packings. No more than $\frac{1}{8}$in (3mm) of tilt is required to make it very noticeable, but it adds a great deal of realism to a layout. Just as a flat road, modelled without camber, would look wrong, so a bold curve without super-elevation fails to look convincing. Touches like this do make a difference.

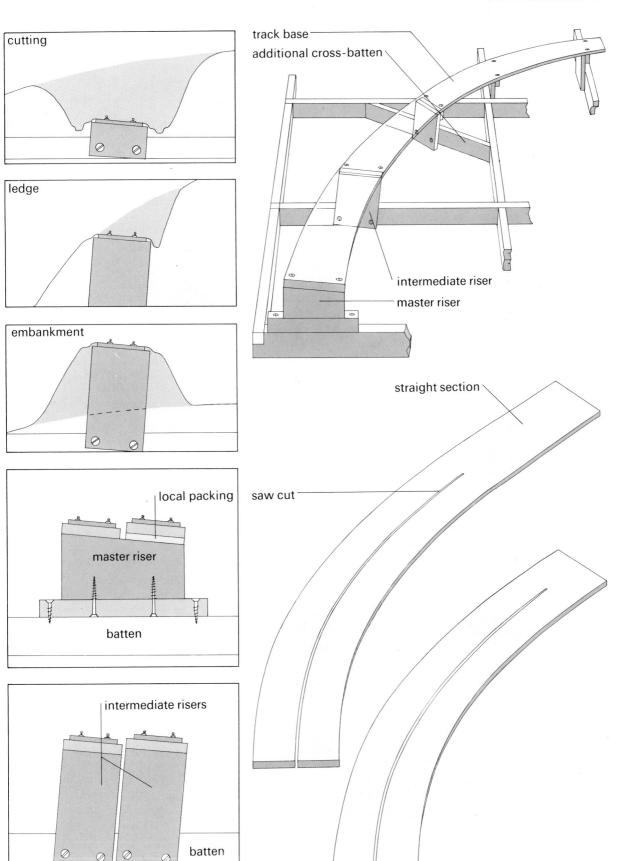

cutting

ledge

embankment

local packing

master riser

batten

intermediate risers

batten

track base

additional cross-batten

intermediate riser

master riser

straight section

saw cut

ends twisted

BASIC TRACK WIRING

Wiring a large model railway differs in only one respect from wiring a simple train set, there is more of it. However, because the larger layout is permanently fixed, the wiring only has to be done once; as a result, it is possible to consider additional features such as automatic control. This is possible, but not advisable, at least in the early stages. At present, all forms of automatic control are rigid, in the sense that one can only do what has been built into the system, though it is probable that, before long, developments in micro-electronics will allow an automatic control device, which can be programmed, to be marketed. The potential exists in the micro-processor, but at present we lack the software and interface systems needed to carry out the commands.

The only purpose of model railway electrification is to allow us to control a train. We can only effectively control one train at a time and no electronic developments can alter this. We shall look at the situation needed to control two trains independently on one layout later, but for the moment, there are two objectives. First, we have to be able to make the locomotive and, with it, the train, move in the direction and at the speed we require. Second, we need to prevent every other locomotive, multiple unit railcar or other form of motive power on the layout from moving at all. This is simpler than it sounds.

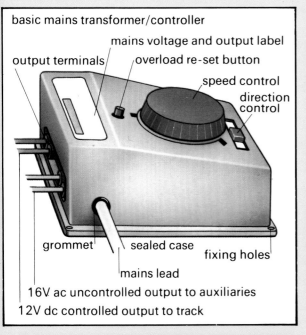

basic mains transformer/controller

mains voltage and output label

output terminals

overload re-set button

speed control

direction control

grommet

sealed case

fixing holes

mains lead

16V ac uncontrolled output to auxiliaries

12V dc controlled output to track

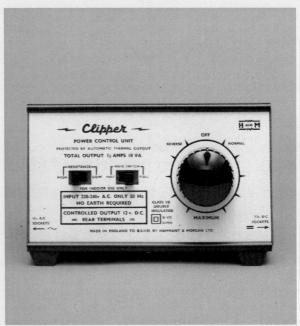

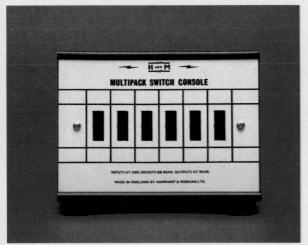

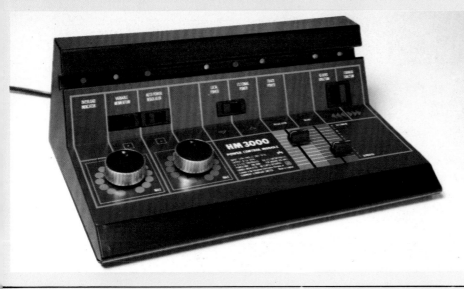

Top left: A basic mains transformer controller.

Top right: An example of a single train controller with ample power for expansion.

Centre left: Switch panels are available in smart consoles as in this HM example.

Centre right: This resistance controller is custom-made for panel mounting.

Below: One of the most up-to-date control modules, capable of simulating the appearance of weight in relation to speed of a prototype by regulating the brake control and speed of the locomotive.

Far left: A selection of electrical components, designed exclusively for railway modelling, which will enable the modeller to carry out basic wiring with confidence and safety.

The control unit

The first stage is to provide a suitable supply of electricity. We require a supply of DC current which can be varied from 0–12-volt, and reversible in polarity. The higher the voltage, the faster the motor in the locomotive revolves, while the polarity of supply determines the direction of travel. We achieve this with a control unit. These come in many types, and have their basic controls arranged in one of three ways. The simplest is the single knob, which is largely preferred in Britain. The single knob, lever or handle has a central 'off' position, and is turned either way for direction; the further you twist it from the off position, the faster the train moves.

The second type, more popular in the USA, has a speed control knob, lever or handle, which is turned clockwise to increase speed, and a separate reversing switch which may have an additional central off position. The third type substitutes a slider for the knob, but is otherwise identical to the second type.

All model railway controllers from reputable manufacturers give good control. More advanced electronic controls give certain features, and, of these, feed-back compensation which ensures that the train travels at a constant speed up or down hill is probably the most useful. Brake and inertia settings can be great fun, but in certain applications, notably shunting, they are often troublesome. Although, however, an advanced electronic controller can get the very best out of a mechanically-sound locomotive fitted with a responsive motor, no amount of solid-state circuitry can transform a poorly-performing model.

One other type of control box can be mentioned, the type that is often included in cheap train sets. The simple battery unit is expensive to operate, and the very small mains-powered device, with a two speed control, is inadequate beyond the elementary toy level. Fortunately, quite good resistance controllers are now being included in the better sets.

Most people begin with self-powered controllers. Providing they have a controlled 0–12-volt output at least 6va or $\frac{1}{2}$A output, they will suffice. It is better to have an additional independent 16-volt AC output for auxiliaries, and the main output should be at least 12va (1A), preferably 20va ($1\frac{1}{2}$A); the latter will take care of double-heading or coach lighting should you wish to include this at a later date.

Mains-powered units produced by reputable manufacturers are made to very rigid specifications. They have to meet the stringent safety requirements of the country where they are sold. Therefore, providing that you ensure that the unit is made by a reputable firm, you will possess a safe device, which will give you reliable control. It is important to purchase a unit made for sale and use in your own country. Quite apart from the question of mains supply voltage and frequency, local specifications must be met. A unit not assembled to the correct specification could invalidate one's household insurance in the event of a fire.

In addition to the completely self-contained units, it is possible to obtain panel-mounted controllers which normally require a 16-volt AC input. These are particularly convenient for building into a control panel, or even into part of the scenery. Furthermore, the heavy transformer can now stand safely on the floor, close to the power socket, with only low voltage wiring taken to the layout.

A third variation is the hand-held controller which frees the operator from having to stop in a single location. It was originally developed for larger lines, where the idea was to follow the train about. It has been found equally attractive for use on small systems, not merely to give ease of working, but to allow the driver to get a different view of his railway. These controllers are usually powered from the AC outputs of existing units, though once the move is made to this type of control, it is sensible to invest in enough special-purpose transformers to do the job effectively.

A large integral mains unit is not only difficult to build into a control panel, but it takes up too much space when placed on the baseboard itself. The favoured solution is to mount a shelf under the baseboard.

Most integral units and transformers have a lead approximately 6ft (2m) long. This is often just too short to reach the socket, and requires an extension. This must be done with a proper connector which is electrically safe; if in doubt get an electrician to extend the lead. On all but the smallest of layouts one usually wants more than one unit, and so it is helpful to connect the wiring for these through a suitable box. The circular type used for extending house lighting circuits is ideal, as it can be screwed to the controller shelf and connected as shown in the diagram. This has been shown with a local switch, which enables one to shut down the model without having to get down to the socket, which is often in a fairly inaccessible place. If this is done, a standard lighting switch mounted in a plastic box is to be preferred, since this will ensure that the live terminals are safely covered. Always take care when handling mains electricity, at best it gives a nasty jolt, but if you happen to be fully earthed, it is usually fatal. If you are in any doubt, do employ a qualified electrician.

Basic wiring theory

Having got a supply of controlled 12-volt DC, we must now connect it to the tracks. First we encounter two-rail wiring theory, which can be made to look remarkably complicated, but as mentioned earlier, the wiring is identical in principle to a normal train set. The subject is relatively straightforward and the following rules explain what has to be done. Straightforward layouts are easily wired in this manner.

1 Take two wires from the power unit to the length of track from which the turnouts radiate. On large layouts several feed points will be needed.

2 You *must* put insulation gaps in each rail where turnouts are back-to-back. Additionally there must always be at least one pair of insulation gaps in any continuous run. These should be made with plastic insulated rail joiners.

3 Term one wire 'feed' and the other 'return'. Any section switches must be in the feed wire; it is advisable to take all feeds independently to the control panel or unit, but all returns can be linked in common.

4 To isolate small sections, e.g. in loco sidings, platform roads etc., place insulated joiners in the feed rail. Bridge the gap thus formed with a pair of wires leading to an on–off switch or a push button.

Reverse loops and triangles

Here we get the situation where the left hand rail meets the right hand rail and, if nothing were done, a short circuit would result. There are several ways round this problem. The simplest and most elegant is to avoid the use of reverse loops and triangles in the first place. It is worth pointing out that the majority of good, successful model railways do not include them; indeed, in practice, they are only of much value on a very large system.

If you wish to use reverse loops and triangles there are two practical solutions. The first is to isolate completely both ends of the loop and to feed the isolated section through a reverse switch. Although this is generally fed from the controller, and as a result the train has to stop, it can be avoided if the loop section is fed from a second, auxiliary control, taking its supply directly from either a 12-volt DC output on the main controller, or from a separate power supply.

In the case of a triangle, it is normal for

The right-hand drawing shows an installation with mains feed to a junction box and two self-contained controllers. On the left is a floor-mounted transformer with 16-volt AC current fed to a panel-mounted controller. Note the shelf mounting for the self-contained controllers and ancillaries.

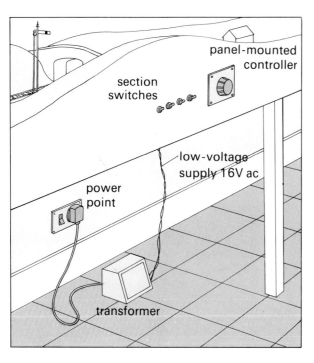

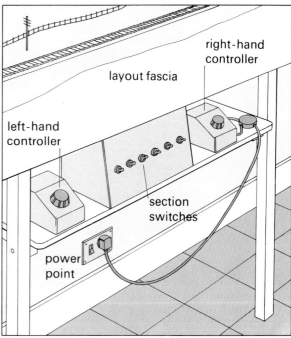

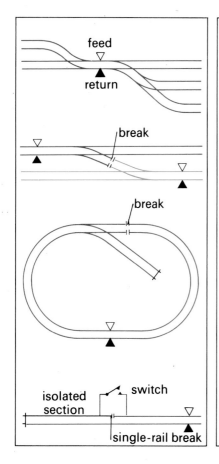

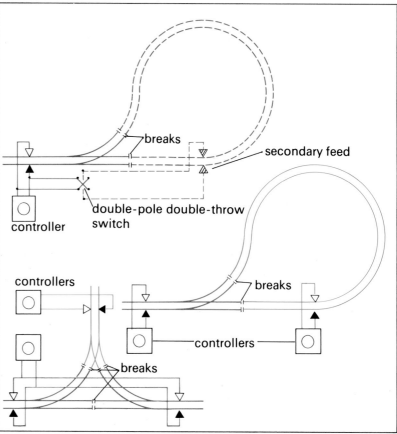

Above: Electrical connections and breaks to isolate sections can sometimes seem a little mystifying to a newcomer. The most frequent instances where changes of polarity or isolating breaks are required are shown here, and most . other functions are combinations of these fundamentals.

Opposite: Wiring diagrams for running more than one train on a double-track loop with sidings. The top diagram uses a double controller and an isolating switch, the centre diagram two controllers and a switchboard, and the bottom one three controllers. Moving a train from a siding is shown on the right.

a terminus to feed a continuous main line. In this instance, the best solution is to have one controller on the main line and another working the terminus. Both controllers have to be set in unison in order to pass a train across the gap.

We spoke earlier of keeping the locomotives stationary which we do not wish to move. This is done by isolation. Most two-rail turnouts incorporate an isolation feature, with the result that when they are set against a siding, any locomotive standing on the siding will not move. In the case of loops, where there are turnouts at each end, it would appear that both turnouts have to be set against the train, but if, as can easily be arranged, the rails of the loop have isolating breaks in them, either end of the loop can be independently isolated. The advantages of this are shown in the diagram where the opposite ends of a single track passing loop are fed from separate controllers. With this arrangement, trains can run into opposing sides of the loop simultaneously, and will come to a halt once they pass the section break. If the turnouts are now reversed the trains can proceed on opposing controllers.

Operating two trains

You will doubtless reach a stage when you wish to operate two trains at once on a single piece of track, and in opposite directions. This can be done on the track arrangement intended to allow them to pass one another, the simple loop.

'Track' is a term with a number of possible meanings, but in this context it is assumed to be a single continuous length of railway line. In order to run two trains under independent control on one single length of line of infinite length complex electronic control is needed. However, it is fairly obvious, particularly if our track is a circuit of reasonable size, that unless both trains are travelling in the same direction at the same speed they are going to collide sooner or later. With normal control, two trains on one continuous circuit of track will travel in the same direction at about the same speed.

However, most newcomers tend to speak of 'track' when they mean the whole 'layout'. To run two trains under independent control on the one layout doesn't call for special electrical arrangements, but it does require proper layout design. The prime

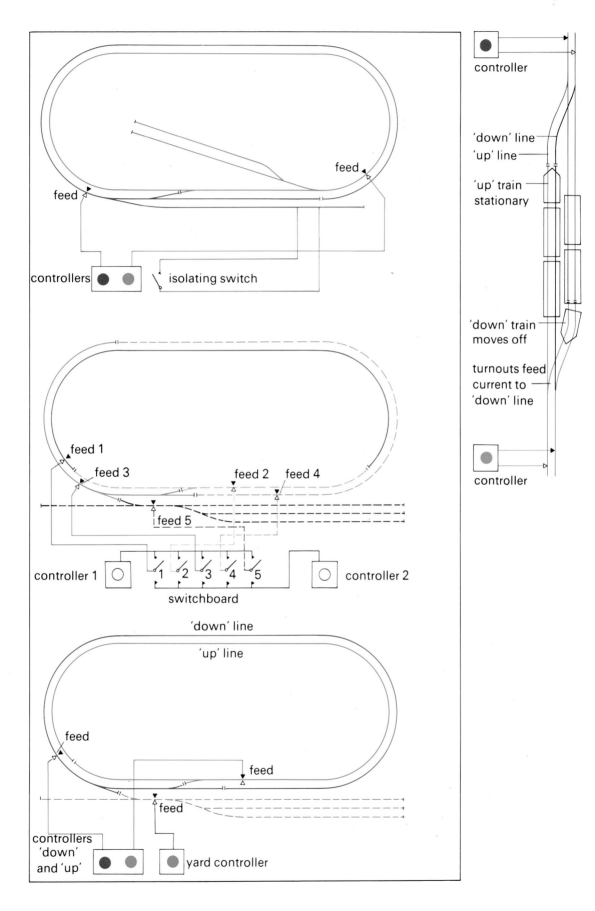

feed

feed

controllers

isolating switch

feed 1

feed 3

feed 2 feed 4

feed 5

controller 1

1 2 3 4 5

controller 2

switchboard

'down' line

'up' line

feed

feed

feed

controllers
'down'
and 'up'

yard controller

controller

'down' line

'up' line

'up' train
stationary

'down' train
moves off

turnouts feed
current to
'down' line

controller

requirement for operating any number of trains under independent control is a layout so designed that each can move at will without actually affecting the movement of any other. For the moment let us look at the simplest possible arrangement, double track main line. Here the arrangement is very simple: you connect one controller to the outer oval and another to the inner oval so that you can run two trains at once.

A slightly more sophisticated layout would have, in addition to the double track, a completely independent goods yard with a shunting neck to permit marshalling. This particujlar design provides a sound, usable model which can be run in a similar fashion to the full-sized system. It requires three controllers: up, down and yard. Paradoxically, one normally uses the best controller on the yard, because while all controllers, even the simplest, are capable of running trains at steady speeds, when shunting one requires the highest precision attainable. With this set-up, the two trains on the main line can run round the track whilst the operator shunts the yard.

However, once the operator has made up a new train and wishes to get it on to the main line, the fun begins! He has not only to get one train off the main line into the sidings, but then get the train from the yard out on to the main line. This could result in having to use all three controllers set in unison. Stopping the trains on the main line presents no great difficulty, provided that one has anticipated the need and provided an isolating section. Good design suggests that these isolating sections on the main line are located against stop signals, so that the process makes sense. This still leaves us with the problem of moving a train across from one controller to another.

However, the layout design will indicate quite clearly that this particular manoeuvre will always take place over the same part of the track. These rails can be fed through a changeover switch so that they can be connected to either the appropriate 'up' or 'down' main line controller or, if the switches are reversed, to the 'yard' control used for shunting, thus removing the need to synchronise controllers.

This is a specialised form of cab control. In certain advanced model railways, where full signalling is provided, and the station has a lever frame or its equivalent, electrical interlocking can be arranged to switch control circuits as the points and signals are moved. Isolating sections are linked to the appropriate stop signals. There are no separate electrical switches. The controller is duplicating the track layout, electrically, with the aid of changeover switches linked to the points and signals. This is not at all complicated in theory, but the end result is extremely complex, resulting in nearly as much wiring as a small telephone exchange. Indeed, much model railway wiring parallels telephone circuitry, with the result that second-hand telephone equipment, of the pre-electronic era, is particularly suited to model railway control. The standard key switch used in many small office telephone switchboards is greatly prized by model railway enthusiasts, as it has plenty of contacts and is made to stand up to a great deal of use, so that even the discards are of superb quality.

A fully-interlocked system, such as has been hinted at, is very attractive for the expert with a liking for electrical complexity, and a good understanding of full-size signalling practice. The arrangement has many virtues, but one serious snag. It is necessary to pull off the appropriate signals before a train will move, so that not only is it necessary to put these signals into the lever frame, and use them, but it is impossible to carry out wrong moves on the model. Unlike the full-sized driver, the operator on such a layout cannot pass a signal at danger. This is a fairly obvious and attractive development in the hobby and the history of model railways has many cases of independent re-invention of this idea. Unfortunately, the inherent snag of this system is that it can go wrong quite easily and render the layout completely inoperative. However, with careful design this can be overcome and is a fascinating challenge for anyone with an interest in electrical wiring.

Cab control

There is also a simpler system which gives a good deal of flexibility without too much complication known as cab control. This, in fact, has nothing to do with the cab of the locomotive; the term came into use because it enabled the operator to move his control area around the layout as though he were in the driver's cab. The principle is that the layout is divided into a number of 'blocks'. These are parts of the layout which are large enough to allow a train to move some distance and to carry out shunting without interfering with the

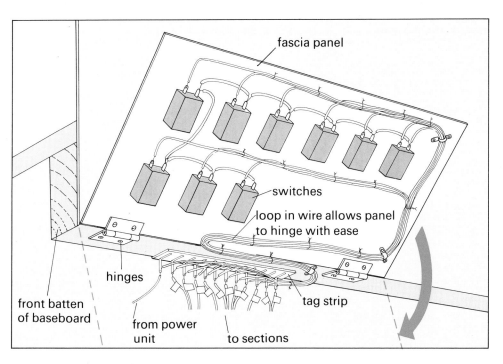

fascia panel

switches

loop in wire allows panel
to hinge with ease

hinges

tag strip

front batten
of baseboard

from power
unit

to sections

Hinged front covers to
control panels allow
easy access to the
wiring on the back of
the panel. Note the
necessity of allowing a
little slack in the wires
and identification tags
attached to all on-
going section wires.
Stapling wires in place
prevents inadvertent
tugs from
disconnecting them.

free movement of another train on an adjacent block. In addition, at station throats and junctions, small key sections which can form links between adjacent blocks are treated as blocks in their own right, even though they cannot be used independently.

Each block is fed independently through a changeover switch. The number of poles in each switch depends on the number of controllers in use. The diagram shows the simplest arrangement, a pair of controllers with two-way centre-off switches for each block. For many layouts, this arrangement is sufficient, permitting two operators to enjoy a good running session and enabling them to cope with most requirements. If an operator tries to run two trains at once, he will probably find that one has to be run on a continuous section of main line, or while he is attending to one, the other will run out of track and be derailed.

At first sight it might seem that double pole switches are required for cab control. However, providing each controller is fed from a separate unit with its own trans-former (or from a twin unit which is described by the manufacturer as suitable for common-return-wiring) only the feeds need to be switched and all returns can be connected.

Electric locomotives

So far, we have only considered steam outline or diesel locomotives, by implica-tion. Electric locomotives and multiple-unit-stock can be operated perfectly well from a standard two-rail system. Indeed, British three-rail stock is generally con-trolled in this way due to the inherent problems of arranging reliable pick-ups on an outside third rail which do not look ungainly. The conductor rail is either absent, or put there for aesthetic reasons only. Overhead supply, which is far and away the most common throughout the rest of the world, is less difficult to omit as it is so very obvious.

When overhead gear has to be erected, it might as well be made operative. Electric locomotives are generally provided with a simple changeover switch to allow the user to select overhead or rail pick up; in such cases one set of track wheels is used as a return. This creates one small problem — the locomotives must never be turned. For this reason, where it is desired to operate an electrified line from overhead *and* the track, reversing loops and triangles may be used. Electric locomotives are best not run on to turntables unless the return side is distinctively marked so that the model can be correctly aligned on leaving the shed.

Dividing an overhead system into sec-tions is apt to get a little complicated, but one advantage of having both overhead and track electrified is that there is indepen-dent control of the electric locomotives. This can get very complicated, so the beginner is advised to start out with a

Overleaf: Part of a large
American layout in $\frac{1}{4}$in
scale (0 gauge) built
by Robert Hegge. Code
100 rail laid on wood
ties (sleepers) with
four spikes per tie,
everything scratch-
built except the model
cars. The Crooked
Mountain Lines layout
represents early 1930s
operation in the USA.
Inset is a diagrammatic
explanation of the
principle of alternative
overhead and track
electrification.

support mast

catenary wire

contact wire

panto-
graph

change-over
switch

motor
brushes

wire
soldered
to rails

baseboard

from
controller 2

from
controller 1

dummy overhead supply and work into independent control slowly.

Wiring for points and signals

So far we have only considered track wiring, which is of course the most essential part. Remote control of points and signals is optional, and is relatively simple.

Point control is almost exclusively carried out with double solenoid motors, either built into the turnouts or supplied as an accessory. These consist of two coils, a central armature and a locking mechanism. A pulse of AC current is sent through one coil, pulling the armature to one side and, through suitable linkage, operating the turnout. It is not proposed to go into the mechanical details, since these are covered in the maker's instructions.

Electrically, there is one common wire, taken to the AC output of the power unit. A lead from the other transformer output is taken to a special switch or push-button unit, then two wires from this switch are taken to the other two terminals of the motor. It is all very simple. There is just one thing to note, and that is getting the direction the point moves for a specific position of the switch correct. The simplest method is to link up the two wires at random, test, and if incorrect (there is a 50 : 50 chance it will not be), you simply reverse the wires.

Electrically-operated signals are similarly wired to the switch if they are of the semaphore pattern. Coloured light signals differ, for here, instead of a pulse, a steady supply is needed, and they are therefore controlled by simple changeover switches. Multiple aspect signals are either worked from a three- or four-way wafer switch or, in more advanced systems, are linked together to show successive aspects.

Organising the wiring

If the actual wiring is carried out in a completely haphazard fashion, the result will be a tangle of wires hidden under the baseboard. Providing each circuit is installed and tested in order, the system will work. However, when something goes wrong, or a circuit has to be altered, tracing the appropriate wire tends to be troublesome. Some people believe that the answer to this is colour coding. In practice, the use of colour-coded wiring tends to break down under the special problems of model railway wiring.

One problem is that a lot of circuits can have dual functions, leading to the need for rather more colours than are readily available. The other far more significant problem is that a layout needs a lot of wire, and it is virtually impossible to calculate exactly how much of each specific colour is needed. As a result, one often discovers that one has run out of, say, white, whilst there is an almost full roll of green. At that point colour coding is apt to be abandoned.

A better system is the wiring book. This is not, however, a wiring diagram. In the wiring book, each wire, from switch to

Double solenoid motors are normal for point operation and can be mounted below the baseboard, connected by a wire crank, or concealed in some item of lineside equipment such as a platelayer's hut. A passing switch can be arranged to trigger the point motor and reset the points.

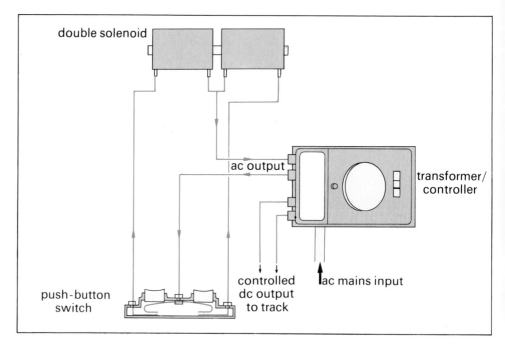

double solenoid

ac output

transformer/ controller

push-button switch

controlled dc output to track

ac mains input

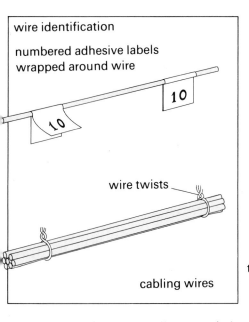

wire identification

numbered adhesive labels
wrapped around wire

10

10

wire twists

cabling wires

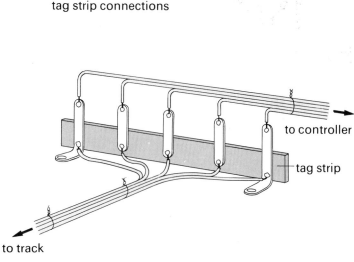

tag strip connections

to controller

tag strip

to track

track section, from controller to switch-board, or whatever, is identified and given a code number. The exact numbering scheme is not important, it doesn't even have to be logical. An inexpensive note-book, ruled in squares, is ideal as a wiring book. The wires are then tagged. There are two methods. One involves the use of self adhesive tabs, obtainable in any large stationers. The codes are written on the tags, at one end, then the tag is folded back on itself around the wire. Two such tags are needed, one at each end. There is little point in identifying a wire halfway along.

This leads to a simpler arrangement, the use of tag-strips. These are strategically located near to the wiring point on the layout and close to the control panel. Each tag is numbered, and the numbering recorded in the front of the wiring book, together with the location of the tag-strip. Then each wire is identified by its two end tags. Connections between tag-strips take the form of cable looms. These can be multi-cored cable, or built up by putting in a wire at a time. This is the one place where colour coding makes sense, since if each wire has a different colour, it is relatively easy to decide which is which.

Connections to the track on a permanent layout are made by bringing the wire up through the baseboard and soldering it into the web of the rail. Alternatively, it is feasible to solder stiff bare wire droppers as shown in the diagram. These project about 10mm below the baseboard surface and form a handy tag to which one may solder the connecting wire. In such cases, it helps to identify the connection with a sticky label.

To avoid sub-baseboard cats' cradles, the wires should be cabled. This involves nothing more complicated than bringing the wires together and binding them with a twist of wire. Professional wiring often uses waxed thread or special plastic clips, both of which are fine when the wiring is going to remain undisturbed. Model rail-way circuitry tends to be in a state of flux, and the wire twist is simple, cheap and easily undone when you need to alter it.

A fair amount of cabling runs along the baseboard from wiring point to wiring point. A series of small hooks screwed into the framing serves to keep the cable looms neat. Multi-core cable can be clipped in place to the framing if preferred. If the baseboard is broken into sections, wiring can be carried across the joint by means of jumper cables and multi-pin plugs and sockets. Portable layouts can have mating sockets as shown in the diagram.

Control panels

It is not difficult to devise very complex looking panels; the addition of panel lights, meters and such devices can rapidly reach a rough simulation of an aeronautical mission control. This is not at all neces-sary, since for most layouts a few simple switches, plus two or three controllers, will suffice. The only reason for having an elaborate panel is that you enjoy building one, and consider the effort worthwhile. It may not add to the operating efficiency of the model, but it impresses visitors!

Tidy wiring reduces maintenance and makes tracing a fault very much simpler. Numbered tags at each end of each wire, with the numbers identified in a wiring book, or connecting to identifiable tag strips, preferably by colour-coded wire, can save hours of checking.

NATURAL SCENERY

Once the trackwork has been completed and wired up, and testing has confirmed that everything works well, then begins the fascinating task of making the layout as realistic as possible. Much will depend on the design of the trackwork and the space available beyond the boundaries 'owned' by the railway company. During the planning stages some thought will have been given to the type of layout and scene which you wish to reproduce. A great deal will also depend on the scale you have chosen. In N gauge (2mm : 1ft) obviously much more space is available for scenery than if 4mm scale were used. Similarly in 7mm scale, little scenic space will be available normally, unless one selects the garden area in which to locate the railway layout.

Above: An 0 gauge layout with scenic work begun by ballasting the track.

Preceding pages: The house and barn featured here are shown in more detail later in the chapter. Part of their impact lies in the bold use of contrasting textures.

Below: Water culverts passing through a rocky embankment.

There is a tremendous variation in natural scenery in the world, whether it is in the British Isles or in one of the larger land masses of North America, Europe, or elsewhere. The modeller needs to be a keen observer of detail. One must try to achieve the natural effect, in order to produce a convincing real life scene. This does not, of course, mean that the natural effect must only be portrayed in fields and villages, for it can equally depict very bleak hill country, a town or city. Scenery exists in a variety of dramatic forms from the flat prairies of Canada or the United States, to the Rocky Mountain landscape which runs through both countries, or the Alps and other mountain ranges in the European continent. A coastal railway gives another opportunity to produce an unusual scenic effect. The Devon coastline in England is very suitable but has been modelled only a few times.

Some modellers believe that scenery is not really necessary, and the prime objective is to run the trains. To them, scenery only takes up valuable track space. Few modellers, however, subscribe to this view. Most people seek to portray a balanced and prototypical scene, as near to the original as possible.

Basic considerations

During the trackwork stage, the broad plan and design for the scenery will have determined whether you work on a flat baseboard or a series of different levels. Perhaps the simplest of layouts will be the one constructed on flat baseboards. This will give a firm base for whatever scenic features are required. However, if during the construction of the baseboard, provision is made for viaducts and bridges, then it is necessary to ensure that the framework for each section of the baseboard is well braced to avoid twisting and warping. It is essential that all scenery is built on a firm foundation, and care should

be taken at all stages. Another consideration is whether the layout is to be of permanent construction and virtually immovable, or planned to be a portable layout built in a number of sections. If it is to be portable then not only will the scenery have to be fairly durable, but it must also be light in weight so that it can be carried easily.

Tunnels and hills

Most model railway layouts have a tunnel entrance at either end of the scenic area as this gives the most complete scenic break possible. Often however, the scenery built over the tunnel is too shallow and both the prototypical and the natural effect is lost. It should be remembered that when the early railway lines were being constructed, a tunnel was one of the most costly structures to make, since progress through solid rock formations was slow and the work was hazardous. Whenever possible, therefore, the ground would be opened out to make a cutting through which the line

could run. A tunnel was only cut where the depth of the hill ahead was considerable and opening out was impracticable. The modeller needs, therefore, to set the tunnel entrance into a solid hill-formation which will dominate the trains using the line, as with the prototype. The tunnel design is selected and constructed over the railway line. Realistic plastic tunnel entrances, which are available in most model shops, can be used instead. The following chapter gives some suggestions on tunnel portals.

Once the tunnel mouth is in place, and the initial painting completed, you can then start on the immediate surroundings. The approach to a tunnel can either be through a quarried rock structure, through sloping embankments, or between brick or stone abutments. Only if you are modelling a particular section of line accurately will the choice be limited to an exact prototype. As a suggestion, scenery at the tunnel entrance should be twice the depth of the tunnel portal, and should continue rising slightly (or more steeply if one

A transition from cutting to embankment demonstrates the basic framing required. Additional contour variations can be created locally by crumpling the chicken wire (also called wire netting). An alternative is to fill in the contours with scrap expanded polystyrene blocks.

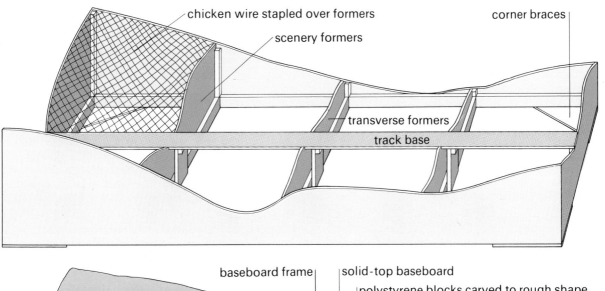

chicken wire stapled over formers

scenery formers

corner braces

transverse formers

track base

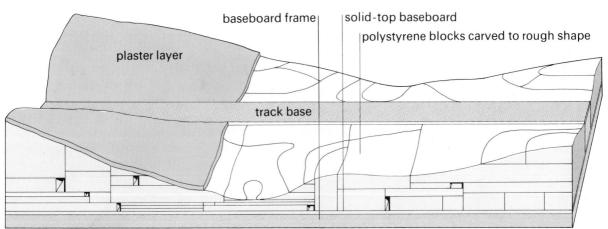

baseboard frame

solid-top baseboard

polystyrene blocks carved to rough shape

plaster layer

track base

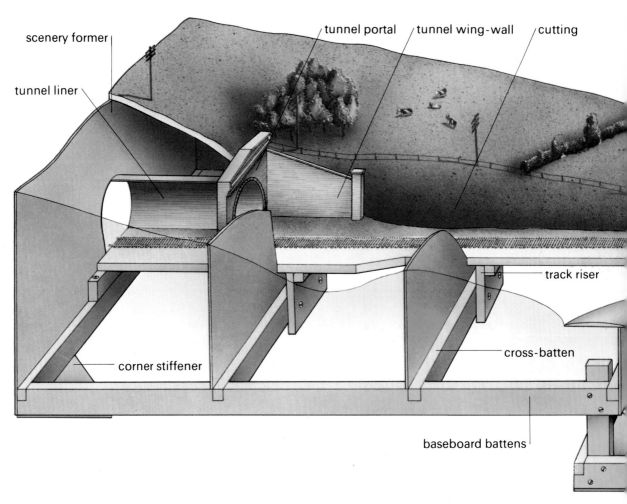

scenery former

tunnel liner

tunnel portal

tunnel wing-wall

cutting

track riser

corner stiffener

cross-batten

baseboard battens

Above: An example of scenic structure embodying a hill with tunnel and wing-walls, a cutting, embankment, road, river and viaduct—all features adding to the attraction of a layout. Smaller details include trees, bushes, telegraph poles, fencing, a level crossing, modern house and cows, again all holding the viewer's interest.

chooses) back from the cutaway vertical point. The edges of the baseboard should be profiled as though the hill has been cut through with a knife. A timber framework is vital to give strength to the hill structure, and to provide a base on which to build. First, the profiles for the edges of the baseboards are cut and screwed or nailed in place. When the timber framework around the tunnel entrance is ready, then fine-mesh chicken wire can be used to cover the area. Staple an edge of the wire to one edge profile, cut, twist and bend the wire to fit around the tunnel entrance and the timber framework adding support battens between the wire and baseboard to give rigidity. Staple or clip the wire to all edges and supports firmly.

There are various methods of ground surface construction recommended, and each in turn has advantages and disadvantages which suit particular purposes. One method uses old fabrics such as bed sheets, shirts and woollen items to cover the wire framework. Contact adhesive is used to attach the cloth. Mod-roc, or a similar

plaster-impregnated material, is then used in small pieces to cover the fabric and wire; Mod-roc is similar to the material used to plaster broken limbs: an open-weave bandage loaded with dry plaster which, when dipped in water, can be smoothed into place over irregular contours and sets hard in a few minutes. It is sold in model shops, but an alternative is simply to mix small amounts of plaster of Paris to the consistency of thick cream and dip into this small pieces of thinnish, open-weave rag which can be draped over the wire. Strips of perhaps 4×12in (100×300mm) will probably be the largest needed; work must be swift as each mix of plaster remains workable for only a minute or two.

Mod-roc pieces can, of course, be dipped in coloured water, or plaster mixed with coloured water, to give the basic scenery colouring. Additional colour can be added during the drying-out stage. Flock powders or lint can also be used to give texture to the structure, with perhaps the best effect for grassland achieved by using

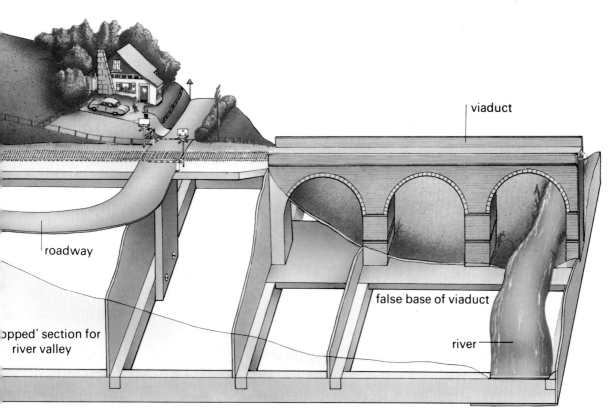

viaduct

roadway

false base of viaduct

opped' section for
river valley

river

green-dyed lint. The lint should be dyed and dried beforehand and, whilst the plaster is still wet, pressed on, and left to dry. Once it is dry, peel off the main thickness of lint to leave a surface resembling blades of grass standing up from the plaster. If the plaster is allowed to dry, then the dyed lint must be pasted with wallpaper paste on one side and pressed on to the plaster base. When dry, peel off as before.

While this is a very widely-used technique for the construction of terrain, it is by no means the only one, or even necessarily the best for all modellers; different people have different preferences. In general, the most realistic results seem to be obtained when a plaster surface is used. However, the material used to produce the basic contours over which the plaster is applied is relatively unimportant, provided that it gives a firm foundation and supports the plaster over the whole area. Trying to fix a tree on unsupported plaster is likely to produce cracking and even sinking, and while a repair is not difficult,

it is a nuisance. If the scenic detail has been planned, it is possible to design bases for later surface additions, leaving the main topography as a relatively light shell.

In recent years, expanded polystyrene has become extremely popular for scenery construction. It can be salvaged from packaging (try a television shop) and is

Below: Chicken wire is used here to form the basis of this typical mountain scene, where the track is laid on a bed cut from the rock wall.

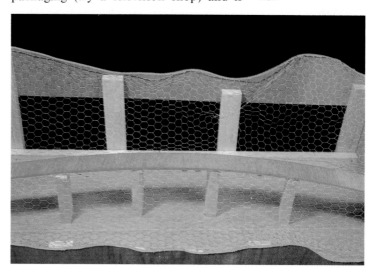

Commercial tunnel portals (right) can be purchased, or made from ply or card.
Expanded polystyrene block, crumpled paper, and a commercial tunnel portal are all that is required to construct a realistic tunnel.

A card insert behind the tunnel mouth ensures a clear track and forms a base for the crumpled paper.
Use ceiling tile adhesive (a latex type) since other glues may dissolve the polystyrene.

Crumpled paper can be held in place with tape while open-weave cloth strips dipped in builders' plaster are laid over. Mix plaster with a 10:1 water/PVA glue solution. Metal foil protects track.

'Butter' crumpled foil with thicker plaster $\frac{1}{4}$in thick, lay in place and peel off foil when nearly set. Paint two coats of matt emulsion, sprinkle while wet with small stones, ballast and grass textures.

Track is laid on cork underlay for quiet running, preferably while wet with thick emulsion or oil paint so that ballast can be sprinkled between the sleepers etc. Take care with points to avoid sticking.

easily broken or cut to suit requirements. It is not essential, incidentally, to use a 'hot wire' cutter for this sort of use, but care must be taken with adhesives and paints. Ceiling tile adhesive or white PVA glue are suitable, and emulsion paint or water-based poster/powder paints are ideal. The very light weight of the polystyrene makes it ideal for portable layouts, yet it is solid enough to give firm support for plaster; once sealed off by the plaster, the type of paint used is unimportant.

Other more economical methods of constructing scenery should also be considered, but while satisfactory results can be achieved by using pasted paper layers, this method is not recommended for portable layouts. Nevertheless the use of paper and papier-maché was popular on smaller single board layouts until expanded polystyrene became available.

For small hills and cuttings, crumpled paper can be glued to the baseboard and strips of paper pasted over it from side to side and criss-crossed. Wallpaper paste is used which, when fully dried out, helps to form a reasonably rigid base on which a thin coating of plaster or pasted lint can be placed. Papier-maché can also be added to areas where a little more rugged surface is required, and when dried out, it can be painted and flocked. Sand mixed into paint and plaster makes convincing earth.

The methods described above can also be used to form scenic undulations around the layout and are not only confined to the

entrances to tunnels. Large areas of land-scape may be necessary to hide from view the trackwork which changes levels or directions, or to cover the so-called 'hidden' storage sidings which are a feature of most model layouts. In these circumstances, then a rigid wooden framework, well-supported from the baseboard, is necessary. Whilst polystyrene blocks can be used for support to replace wooden battens, the chicken-wire mesh method is strongly recommended.

Larger hills are best made with a foundation of wooden boxes firmly glued and screwed in place, with the contour formers secured to them. With a little ingenuity, and access arranged from the back or side, quite a lot of storage space can be created inside the boxes. Another use for the space inside a hill is to build a spiral of track so that a train enters a tunnel at the base of the hill and emerges, after a delay, at a different level and in a different direction. The climb inside the hill need not be to a scale gradient, but the fall of track from the

high point back to baseboard level should be. It can be disposed throughout the layout, giving opportunities for bridges, embankments and other scenic details. Access to the track within the hill is of course necessary.

Such a feature is, it must be admitted, not entirely true scale, but since the length of a track and the radii of curves etc. are compressed, it can be held to be a legitimate way of compressing level changes unobtrusively. Changes of level add interest and possibilities to a layout, but are difficult to achieve without some such subterfuge, though those enthusiasts whose interest is in prototypical running might well disapprove.

Embankments

Embankments are another railway feature and were built up during the construction of the railway in order that low-lying areas of land or dips in the ground could be traversed without significant changes of track level. Their use in the model railway

A Flying Scotsman by Hornby emerging from the tunnel in the completed scene, which represents a chalk cutting. Trees, bushes and telegraph poles have been added for extra interest. Sketches made on the spot at such a tunnel mouth will help to achieve a natural look.

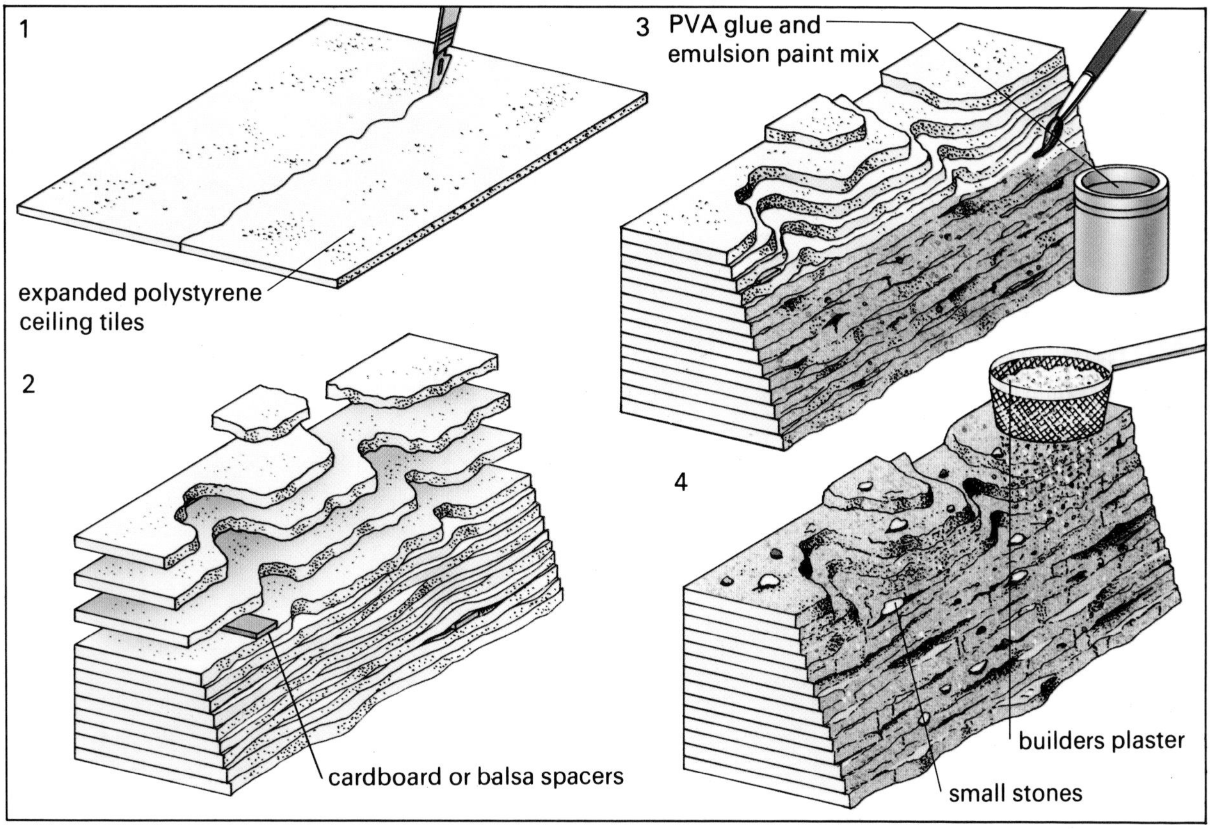

1

expanded polystyrene
ceiling tiles

2

cardboard or balsa spacers

3 PVA glue and
emulsion paint mix

4

builders plaster

small stones

scene can be an advantage, for they emphasise the presence of the railway in a layout and catch the eye. It is, however, necessary when constructing the baseboards for the layout to make the framework extend below the normal level (usually waist height) and use a narrow piece of wood to carry the track across the low level. Wood is recommended for this purpose, not chipboard, unless the latter is well supported. An embankment can be shallow or deep, can extend away from a rock face, or can carry the line to a viaduct or bridge and over meadowland, a river or stream, or merely a roadway. The choice is endless.

It is advisable to study photographs of railway prototypes to achieve realism, particularly when working on embankment structures. In many cases a path ran alongside the ballasted track for the railway platelayer to walk along. In addition there would usually be an area of wild grass, rather like a grass verge to a road, before the edge of the embankment dropped away. Signals and telegraph posts were also often set into this grass area. When selecting the wooden board to take the trackwork on the embankment, allow sufficient width to include them.

Chicken wire mesh or the type of insect screening used for windows is again used to form the embankment, either directly to the framework edge of the baseboard, or to a lower level board which may be required for an area of meadowland. Expanded polystyrene blocks can also be used to form the embankment structure, and the methods of finishing the scenery previously explained can also be used to complete the embankments. There are a number of embankment features which call for attention to detail. Drainage is seldom a problem, but in embankments across meadows, culverts for water drainage or cattle creeps are sometimes constructed. These are often small brick or stone-built tunnels from one side to the other, or simply a drainage pipe to carry water through the embankment. A water drainage line can sometimes be seen on the side of an embankment, where the rainwater has drained down and washed narrow channels a few inches deep into the side. Coarse grasses and small bushes are often found along the sides of embankments, but trees are usually found only at the base. Small bushes and grass roots give a bond to the otherwise loose materials forming the embankment, and while a tree would also do this, a tree swaying in the

Above: Constructing a rock wall from laminations of expanded polystyrene, which could be ceiling tiles. Irregularities can be introduced by random packing strips between layers. After painting, fine stones and crumbled dry plaster can be sieved on to the wet paint and coloured later.

Opposite: A Chesapeake and Ohio locomotive by Bachman standing in front of a rocky bluff constructed by the method shown above. Long runs of such rock walls could be made of almost any scrap material simply faced and topped with random laminations cut from polystyrene sheet.

wind could soon undermine the side of an embankment and cause erosion leading to the trackbed sinking.

If it is decided to include an embankment in your railway layout, why not add an extra touch of realism associated with the steam era of railways? After applying the grass and bushes, give an area an overall spray of dark brown and black, using matt paints, to simulate an embankment which has been on fire. During summertime there were many occasions when sparks from a passing locomotive would ignite an area of lineside, leaving a scorched patch, in fact lineside fires are not entirely unknown in today's diesel era.

Cuttings

Cuttings through small hills are another standard feature of railways running through irregular country, and the methods described earlier apply to the construction of these. Depending on the type of ground, the angle of the banks may vary and sometimes small walls are built along the base. Grassy cuttings are often patterned by bricked-over drainage channels (quite a challenge to reproduce convincingly) and may be overgrown with bushes and small trees, the roots of which assist in preventing slips which could block the line.

Very rough rock faces are found in areas like the English Peak District, Scotland, and of course in many places in Europe and America, and for small areas, cork bark is extremely useful. This can be obtained from model shops or florists and usually has a very rugged surface; any un-rocklike crevices can be filled with plaster and toned in for colour after it is secured in place. For larger rock faces, it is more economic to build a wood or polystyrene backing, surfaced with either plaster carved to shape when 'green' (i.e. set but not bone-hard) or creased thick paper, which when painted can give an excellent effect.

In rugged cuttings, the sides often have large areas which appear to be permanently wet, or have moss and algae well spread around. These effects are reproduced by using lichens, coloured flocks, and clear varnish to give a wet effect. If the effect of water running down the side of a cutting is required, then apply a liberal brush full of varnish to the topmost point and allow to run down. An hour later, repeat the brush full, repeat again one hour

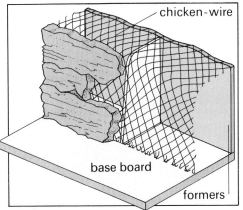

chicken-wire

base board

formers

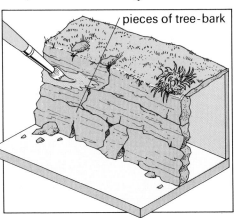

pieces of tree-bark

Left: An alternative method of constructing a rock wall using bark, which has a surface texture ideal for the purpose but usually needs roughly painting over with appropriate colour. Bottom drawing shows dribbling varnish down the face to represent water runs.

later, and repeat until the desired effect has been achieved, perhaps thinning the varnish in later coats sufficiently to allow it to run more easily. Pools of water lying on the path alongside the track are not uncommon, and again clear gloss varnish will give this effect.

In all scenic work it is essential that man-made structures, i.e. bridges, embankments, tunnel entrances etc., are put in place before the scenery work is added, otherwise it will be necessary to undo part of the completed work and patch up afterwards.

Opposite: This Welsh slate quarry is part of a club project by the South Essex branch of the 009 Society. This enthusiast area of model railways uses 4mm scale vehicles and buildings but N gauge (9mm) track to reproduce narrow gauge railways, often found in industrial usage such as mining and quarry work.

Suggestions for the construction of viaducts follow in the next chapter, and there is also some advice on quarries. However, the methods of scenery construction also apply to quarry sites and here the aim is to achieve a stone-face effect, either by carving cast plaster blocks, expanded polystyrene, or cork bark, although this last material is perhaps the one least likely to give the best effect. It should be remembered that all types of geological materials are quarried—sandstone and limestone, granite and iron ore, and in some instances there will be the dark traces of coal. There are quarries in most countries, usually not far from towns, and if you choose to include one, it is worth making arrangements to visit your local quarry, making sure that you are guided as they are dangerous places!

Water features

Rivers and streams are further features which are popular with modellers. Again, provision for the width of a river must be made during the construction of the baseboard stage. The bed must be below normal baseboard level, and if the trackwork is on the normal baseboard, and not above it on an embankment, then several inches must be allowed for the river to run beneath the railway. A bridge will be required for the line, and supports will extend into the river banks or the river itself; the feasibility of the latter will depend on what material the water will be made from. The river level will normally be fairly low, but there should be sufficient space beneath a bridge to allow for higher water and the passage of at least small rowing boats, so make sure that the river gets full consideration at the planning stage. Bear in mind, too, that a small river raises fewer problems than a large one!

A river bed is rarely perfectly flat, so that unless a painted wood or hardboard surface is to be used (and with skill this can look very good) once the river bed's baseboard is in place, a sloppy mixture of plaster should be poured in and ridged and contoured in a random way. Lichen and scraps of foam rubber can be added while the mixture is still wet, and small washed stones, rounded for preference, can be pressed in to represent the rocks and boulders often seen in rivers. Dark greens and browns can be used to colour the river bed and add to an illusion of depth.

The choice of water surface should now be considered. It used to be common to use a sheet of glass, supported on wood strips to be an inch or so above the river bed but still below the level of the surrounding baseboards. The banks can be irregularly shaped, running out over the glass to avoid the necessity of cutting a winding piece of glass. At one time rippled glass used to be used, but this was never very convincing even if used smooth side up. A better proposition is to use a sheet of stiff clear plastic, since this can be cut (for bridge piers etc.), drilled for rushes and other flora, and even dragged up into ripples downstream of bridge supports by using a soldering iron at low heat; experiment on a scrap piece of the plastic first.

Alternatively, the water can be built up with layers of varnish or clear polyester resin. Varnish tends to form a skin if applied thickly, and this slows up the drying as well as allowing shrinkage to form wrinkles, so that building up any depth with a succession of thin coats is a time-consuming process. On the other hand, resin may attack the paints used on the bed or on any weeds, old prams and the like which may be included. Normal resin heats up as it cures, enough to distort

Top left: A sandpit work area including a pond and tree stumps sunk in place in an American H0 scene. Inclusion of derelict or industrial areas adds authenticity to a railway—few pass only through unspoiled countryside.

Bottom left: Coloured sprinkles such as flock powder, dyed sawdust or powdered cork, natural materials such as bark and lichens, and a host of other aids to producing scenic effects are packaged for model railway enthusiasts.

Below: Rivers are interesting to model and add enormously to the attraction of a layout. Clear cold casting resin produces the most convincing result and can be poured in one operation for shallow water.

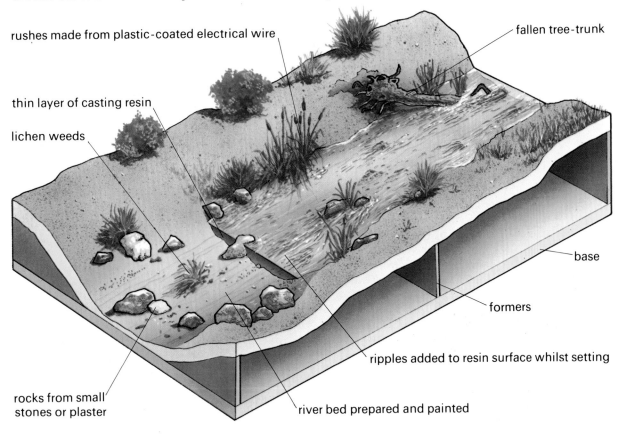

rushes made from plastic-coated electrical wire

fallen tree-trunk

thin layer of casting resin

lichen weeds

base

formers

ripples added to resin surface whilst setting

rocks from small stones or plaster

river bed prepared and painted

A small station and scenic detail on the Arcadia layout built by Martin Brent, a member of the Waterford EM Society. 'EM' stands for 'eighteen millimetres', a more accurate rail gauge for 4mm 00 scale trains than the more common 16.5mm used by most manufacturers.

plastics, though the more expensive cold casting resin used for encapsulating flower or insect specimens does not create problems. Resin can be applied in layers of about $\frac{1}{4}$in (6mm) at a time, giving the opportunity of introducing submarine foliage or even miniature fish. The surface of either varnish or resin can be dragged as it dries and later speckled with white paint to give the effect of turbulence.

Weeds can be cut from plastic card sheet, or a more suitable material, very thin brass sheet. This material will bend and twist to shape more easily and permanently than plastic card and a wire stem can be soldered to give it rigidity. The wire stem can also be soldered to a brass pin set into the bed of the river. Similarly, bulrushes can be reproduced by using plastic

covered wire and stripping all but a small piece of the plastic sheath away. Attention with a small file will soon produce the rounded end top to the plastic, and a small slide of the plastic will allow the wire to protrude sufficiently—no more than $\frac{1}{2}$mm—to give the spike to the top of the bulrush. Painting and fixing in position is all that is required. Rushes can be made from the multi-strand wire easily obtainable at model and electrical shops. Two or more of the strands can be glued or soldered together if required.

Landscapes are rarely empty of people and animals so remember to include some figures. A platelayer walking the track with his long-handled hammer over his shoulder is one addition, and animals will be essential for the grassland areas. The

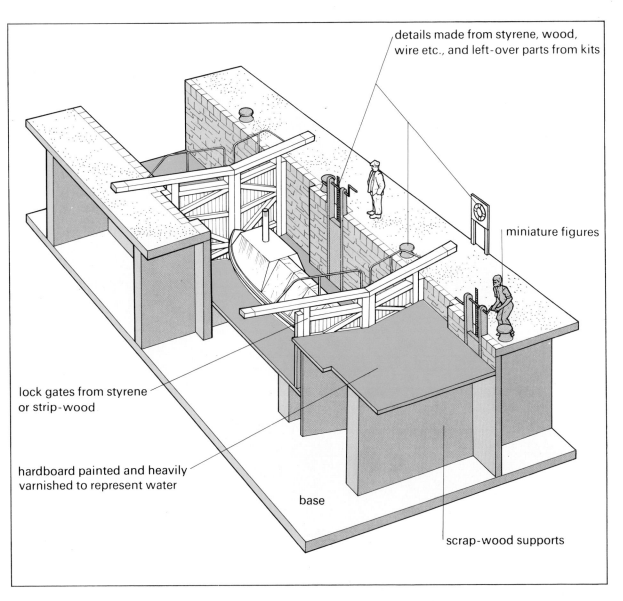

details made from styrene, wood, wire etc., and left-over parts from kits

miniature figures

lock gates from styrene or strip-wood

hardboard painted and heavily varnished to represent water

base

scrap-wood supports

riverside calls for the addition of a fisherman with rod, possibly even standing in the river wearing waders. An umbrella, wicker basket and seat will need to be placed on the bank. If the river bank is sufficiently long, then more than one fisherman can be positioned.

While dealing with rivers and streams, it is appropriate to make reference to the inclusion of canals in a railway layout. It is perhaps not widely known that the British pre-nationalisation railways owned large stretches of canals. This was, of course, a means of transportation in many countries long before the birth of the railways. Canals were man-made and there are many stretches of inland waterway which are actually above the level of the surrounding countryside, albeit contained within wide and solidly-built banks. This feature therefore lends itself well to the model railway scene, for, not only were there canal and railway wharves for the interchange of goods, but it would not be incorrect for a canal to be built on the baseboard with the water level higher than the surrounding area. This could be grassland or the outskirts of a town or village. In fact, with the inclusion of sets of lock gates, then the canal can change levels even to the point where an aqueduct is included. There is considerable choice, and with care and attention to detail an attractive scenic effect will be achieved.

As some of the canals were little used, the water surface can be sprayed brown or green to give the stagnant appearance which is so often a feature of areas of water

Above: Locks of the type illustrated are typical of English canals, but the general principles apply to the often larger Continental locks. Canals have a barely perceptible current and are frequently sheltered, creating a still surface which can be quite reasonably represented with paint and varnish.

Overleaf: Helicopter-eye view of a house nestling in trees on a layout by Peter Buddle of Antler Designs.

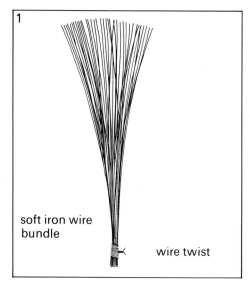

1

soft iron wire bundle

wire twist

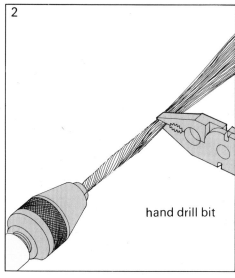

2

hand drill bit

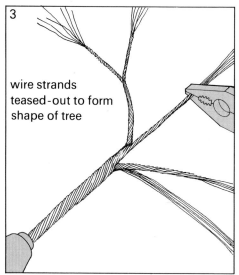

3

wire strands teased-out to form shape of tree

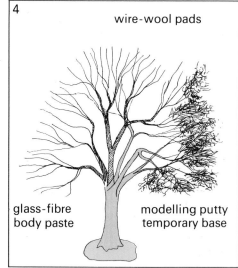

4

wire-wool pads

glass-fibre body paste

modelling putty temporary base

with no natural current. Rubber tyres and other partly submerged objects will also add realism to the canal scene. A number of British railway companies also operated their own canal narrow boats for coal and other freight, and there are kits available to build a typical craft. It is unlikely that original drawings of railway-owned canal boats now exist and it is probable that each one was varied in some way. Modellers' licence therefore dictates that a kit-built boat will suffice. Modellers of the LMS Railway scene may like to know that the Company's canal boats carried their own particular colour scheme.

Trees and hedges

Once the basic ground surface has been completed, attention can be turned to the inclusion of trees, fences, hedges and stone

walls. There are a variety of ways in which each of these can be made up.

There are tree kits available which vary from a simple plastic kit of parts in the Britains Tree series, to those which require much more work to complete. The Britains trees are easy to make up and it is advisable to glue the branch and trunk parts together. With plastic body filler, the joints can be obliterated and, when the filler is dry, a coat of brown and/or black paint, applied patchily, should be sprayed or brushed on. The top edges of branches close to the tree trunks should be given a few brush strokes of dark green paint to represent the green mosses often found on the larger varieties of trees. The plastic leaf pieces are rather uninteresting and the appearance can be improved. Using a pair of pliers, tear small pieces of the plastic

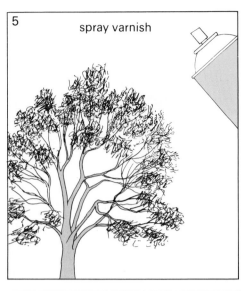

5 spray varnish

6

Left: Two simple methods of representing trees, one using a bunch of wires with foam rubber, both in pieces and grated, and flock powder, suitable for most deciduous trees (Nos 1–6). The second (crêpe paper and wire) approach (Nos 7–8) sounds unpromising, but produces excellent fir trees if shaded crêpe paper is used.

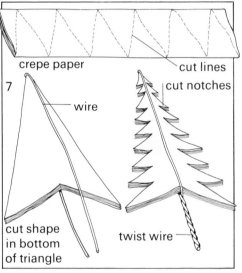

crepe paper

7

wire

cut lines
cut notches

cut shape
in bottom
of triangle

twist wire

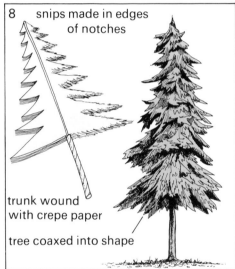

8 snips made in edges
of notches

trunk wound
with crepe paper

tree coaxed into shape

Below: Different geographical areas are often characterised by different trees, so check on forestry books to establish the correct sizes for the types of trees appropriate to a layout. The half-dozen examples drawn show considerable variation of average sizes; the redwood or sequoia is of course limited to N.W. America.

leaves away. Paint beneath the leaf pieces with darkish green and allow the paint to dry. The top surface should then be painted. Whilst the paint remains wet, a light sprinkling of several shades of green flock powder over the paint will do much to improve the leaf texture. Allow the paint to dry before fixing each leaf piece to the branches, again using glue to make the joint permanent. A darker shade of green and shades of brown paint should be applied to the joint and along the plastic leaf stem. This work should do much to improve the appearance.

Another well-tried method is to use multi-strand electrical cable to form the trunk of a tree, with the strands forming branches at varying levels up the trunk. Soldering at the branch points is necessary, but the lower part of the trunk can be

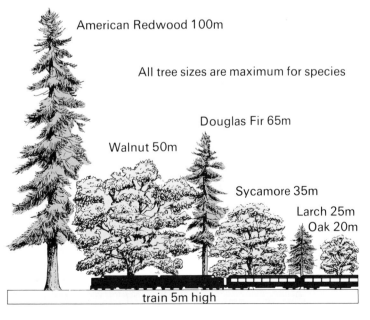

American Redwood 100m

All tree sizes are maximum for species

Douglas Fir 65m

Walnut 50m

Sycamore 35m

Larch 25m
Oak 20m

train 5m high

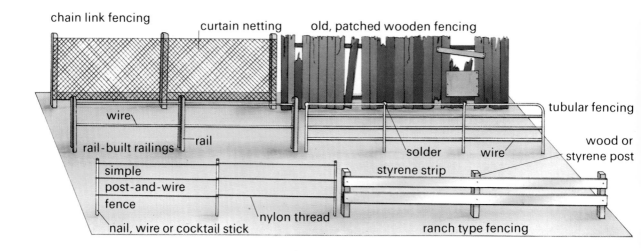

chain link fencing

curtain netting

old, patched wooden fencing

tubular fencing

wire

rail-built railings

rail

solder

wire

wood or styrene post

simple
post-and-wire
fence

styrene strip

nail, wire or cocktail stick

nylon thread

ranch type fencing

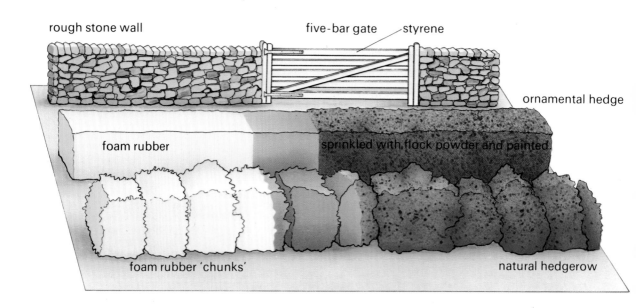

rough stone wall

five-bar gate

styrene

ornamental hedge

foam rubber

sprinkled with flock powder and painted

foam rubber 'chunks'

natural hedgerow

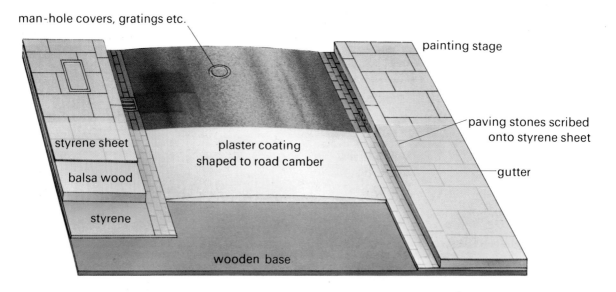

man-hole covers, gratings etc.

painting stage

styrene sheet

balsa wood

styrene

plaster coating
shaped to road camber

paving stones scribed
onto styrene sheet

gutter

wooden base

thickened by soldering on additional pieces of wire. The trunk 'wire' can then be rubbed with Plastic Padding (as used on motor cars) until the wire is no longer discernible. When dry, the trunk can be painted in a mixture of browns, black and shades of dark green. Ideally the wire to use is multi-core, with each individual core made up of many fine strands twisted together. The wires can then be splayed open at the ends to give a fan of fine branches. These branches should have an adhesive applied to the top edges only and then be dipped into flock powder or fine pieces of grated foam rubber. A somewhat unusual alternative method is to use the seeds of nemesia flowers. These are almost like small pieces of paper of uniform size and are light fawn in colour, almost an autumn shade. Varying shades of green can then be sprayed on to the top surface

of these seeds, whilst the underside retains the characteristically lighter natural shade. The spray-painting requires great care, and it is preferable to use a quick-drying cellulose paint (similar to paint for re-touching car bodies). It should be remembered that beneath older trees, large gnarled roots appear and disappear beneath the surface. Because this area is almost always in the shade and rarely has a good soaking of rain, little will grow and the ground surrounding a tree is therefore usually a brown soil colour. Fallen leaves can also be represented in model form.

Other methods of making trees use natural plants to form the basic trunk and branches. The garden or a hedgerow, especially in autumn, should provide many ideas. Privet is an excellent source of twiggy bits for, say, elm or ash trees, and a most useful weed is milfoil, found wild in

Opposite: Fences, walls, hedges and roads need to be in character with their surroundings. Quite a variety can be purchased ready-made or they may be hand-made. It is even possible to buy scale barbed wire! Avoid using constant colours on roads and hedges.

Below: Those seeking the unusual might well consider a snow scene. This is easily achieved by brushing runny white plaster on branches, window ledges etc and spraying overall, from one direction, with 'Christmas snow'.

Another EM scene, this time of a Cornish quayside by Iain Rice. Such a scene incorporates various types of stonework, walling and ground surfaces, as well as allowing scope for ship or boat modelling and the inclusion of lobster pots, fish boxes and other appurtenances of fishing activity.

the countryside. Soaking in cellulose lacquer will prevent most plants from losing too much strength as they dry out. A dyed loofah is excellent for basic foliage, and dried tea leaves or sawdust dyed in a variety of greens then mixed together can be sprinkled over the loofah fibres after spraying them with adhesive, or brushing gum over the top surfaces. Natural mosses and lichens, such as reindeer moss, can also be useful, though they may tend to turn brown and should be colour-sprayed. Artificial lichens which have a rubbery texture avoid this problem.

Mountainous scenes usually need trees of the fir family, and surprisingly successful ones can be made from dark-green crêpe paper. About twenty triangles should be trapped in a long hairpin of soft wire, the ends of which can be wrapped in gummed paper to form the trunk. Notches are cut in all the triangles, almost up to the wire, and the edges of the notches are snipped with scissors. The paper triangles are then separated and spread round, ruffled to fill as much space as possible. Some variation in the paper colour is helpful, but avoid too light a green.

Hedgerows are usually several feet thick and little can be seen through the growth. The rubber lichens or loofah are suitable for hedgerow modelling and small pieces can be fixed with adhesive to the base-board and pressed as close together as desired. Similarly, other pieces can easily be placed on top of the first layer to give height. Hedges are not a constant width, so vary the thickness of those on your layout. When the hedge is constructed, a brush of adhesive along the sides and the top (not necessarily full coverage) and a sprinkling of flock powder will add the finishing touch.

Walls and fences

Stone walls are rather more difficult and time-consuming to build up from scratch, and most people will opt for one of the plastic or plaster moulded stone wall sections available. However, the ballast used by 7mm (0 gauge) modellers can be used for stone wall construction in the smaller scales. This can either be built up stone by stone, or moulded. A balsa wood trough of, say, 6in (150mm) length should be made, and the ballast pieces placed inside. A colourless adhesive is then brushed on and a further layer of stones put on top, with another brush of adhesive applied before it is left to dry. This method will be suitable where the wall is to sit on a flat baseboard, but if the scenic terrain is undulating, then the only convincing option may well be to build the wall stone by stone. Remember, too, that small bushes and plants often grow out of walls and these can be reproduced by using lichens.

There are various fence formations available in model shops and most modellers will, with the aid of plastic card, be able to build a fence to a particular design, that is if a commercially made one is not available.

Roads

Roads need little explanation. Country roads were often cambered from the centre, even the narrowest of lanes, simply to allow rainwater to drain off quickly, and country lanes rarely have white or yellow lines painted down their centres. Town roads, however, have an abundance of road markings which again most modellers will be aware of. Don't forget to include the grass verges before the hedge or wall is positioned. The colouring of worn tarmac tends to be in lighter shades of grey, whilst chippings or gravel have areas of tar on the surface as a result of heavy traffic and the effect of hot summer sun.

Whilst the preceding advice has, in general, applied to modelling the British railway scene, the methods of construction apply just as much to those who are modelling any of the European or North American railways. A prairie scene, where the railway runs through vast areas of flat corn fields, will be easy to construct since there will be no bridges, hills or mountains and only the occasional streams. By contrast a model railway set in the mountainous Rockies or Alps will rely heavily on the rugged appearance of the mountainsides. In a limited area, or on a portable layout, this effect is difficult to achieve. The larger the scale modelled the greater are the difficulties in achieving a convincing result. N gauge undoubtedly has great potential. One way of obtaining a true scale appearance for a mountainous Canadian or American prototype is to lower the baseboards below the usual waist height, preferably to only about 6in or 12in (15–30cm) above the floor. Baseboards of varying levels can, of course, be used if inclines or changes of level are desired. Even though the narrow N gauge track is used, the boards should preferably be a minimum of 2ft (60cm) wide. Individual sections of framework can be constructed

and the 'mountainside' added over fine wire mesh. These sections should be at least 3ft (1m) off the floor, and when placed alongside the track, the line is viewed from above, just as though one is looking down from the mountain tops. The small scale stock adds to the illusion. The mountain sections of scenery can be bolted to the baseboard, or more easily plugged in place with dowels to enable the layout to be fully portable. A study of photographs of a mountainous area will show that above the normal ground-level vegetation, forestry areas are cultivated; above these little will grow. There is almost certainly a well-defined snow line in mountainous regions.

Most modellers portray a scene bathed in sunshine. Some are ingenious enough (and have the time) to illuminate their trains and buildings so that room lights can be turned off, creating a night-time scene. Seldom, though, does anyone ever try to reproduce a winter scene with snow and bare trees. This type of scene would certainly complement the colours of the trains on the line, and it should not be too difficult to achieve. Plaster can be left largely uncoloured, except for vertical surfaces and perhaps vehicle and animal tracks. Trees may not require leaves, walls and hedges and buildings can be sprayed with white paint or the spray-on Christmas snow decoration, and in this way an unusual and attractive model railway scene will develop.

Finally, the sky also has a place in all layouts. Those in a permanent location will have wall space suitably painted, whilst a portable layout without a backdrop will have to rely on one's imagination for a sky effect. In a clear sky the deeper blues will be above one's head, and will fade away further into the distance. Drifting clouds will be less prominent than sharp crisp cumulus clouds, but in modelling a scene it is perhaps best not to have an overpowering sky effect.

Paints

Unless surfaces are wet, there is very little shine in natural objects, especially when reduced in scale. Always, therefore, use matt paints, which can be flat oils, emulsions, or water-mixed powder and poster colours. Use subdued tints; bright colours are the exception rather than the rule. The rest is a matter of personal skill and artistic interpretation!

BUILDINGS AND RAILWAY STRUCTURES

The choice of buildings for your model railway scene will be determined by the type of layout you are intending to construct. In the planning stage of your railway, you will have formed your own ideas on which type of scene you wish to reproduce. It is possible that your views will perhaps be influenced by knowledge of a particular railway location, or by having read of, or viewed, someone else's model scene. Your railway will be *your* interpretation of an original scene on a real railway. It does not matter whether you are using N gauge, proprietary equipment, or the finest handbuilt models, your railway will reflect your views and your attention to detail. Irrespective of the trains you run, the scenery is very important, because, if you stop to think about it, anyone who is viewing your model railway will be looking intently at the scenery, so why not make every effort to make it appear to be as realistic as possible?

Preceding pages:
Steam locomotives
needed a regular
supply of water, and
the style of the water-
towers associated with
various railways is just
as characterful as the
locomotives
themselves.

It is important to remember that the scenery, hills, streams and other natural effects were there long before railways were built and, therefore, the natural terrain of your railway location should be planned. Once the trackwork has been decided, you will need to consider whether the scene is going to be country, a small town or village, or even an industrial area. You

alone can decide but certainly to begin with it is not advisable to try and include all types of area. At this stage you will probably have visited other model railway layouts, either those built by friends or shown to the public at exhibitions. You will, therefore, have seen the standards which have been achieved by others, and it is possible to achieve high standards in

miniature modelling. It is certainly a sound idea to look at other people's work, for this will not only give ideas for types of scene and buildings you might be able to use, but it will stimulate you to work to achieve a high standard through attention to detail and care in construction. As your layout evolves, so the standard of your models will improve, and it is worth remembering that you can always replace an early model at a later date if you choose to do so.

Besides looking at other people's work privately or at exhibitions, try to visit some of the museums which are famous for their achievements. There are few, if any, in the United Kingdom to better the Pendon Museum in the village of Long Witten-ham, near Abingdon, or the Millersdale

Something can always be learned from other people's scenic work, by studying what exactly has achieved the overall effect. Even if something seems not quite right, how it might be improved leads to creative thinking.

Often the approach to a city terminus is between the backs of rows of terraced or semi-detached houses, usually with small gardens, offering limitless scope for a modeller's imagination. In many cases the fronts of the houses need to be modelled too; study an area typical of your layout. Modelled by Peter Buddle.

panorama in the Matlock Bath Model Museum in Derbyshire. In Europe, the Swiss Transport Museum in Lucerne has a superb reproduction of the Gotthard Line, while the American scene is portrayed in the Josephine Randall Junior Museum in San Francisco by the Golden Gate Model Railroaders. There are, of course, other museums in various parts of the world which house model layouts built to a very high standard, and if you are able, maybe while on holiday, to visit one or more of these centres it could prove very worthwhile.

In Britain, the thatched cottages of the Vale of the White Horse as modelled by Roye England and the Pendon team are truly magnificent, while the quarried limestone faces and the magnificent man-made viaducts set into the Derbyshire countryside around Millersdale station are perfect replicas in miniature. Both these centres

have much to interest the British modeller. It quickly becomes apparent that research and accurate recording of details will do much to ensure that the scenery and buildings in your layout become authentic replicas. Research and recording of details will not be accomplished overnight, but spend as much time studying as you can: if possible, photograph your subject. Do not forget that former railway employees in the local population can often describe aspects of the railway scene long since forgotten, but nevertheless important. It is also worth mentioning that a beautifully-modelled section of townscape can be seen in the Madder Valley layout, which is also housed at Pendon Museum.

The constructional points which follow in this chapter apply just as much to foreign railways as to the British scene, since they are not aimed at constructing one specific model building, but achieving

a high standard in all buildings, whatever style these may be.

If the layout is to be an industrial landscape, a station, platform and other buildings directly associated with the Railway Company will need to be built first. Then it will be necessary to incorporate a number of non-railway buildings such as warehouses and shops. If, however, the aim is a village or small town, it will be important to ensure that the balance between the railway and the private buildings is broadly in line with the prototype scene depicted so that one does not overpower or exclude the other.

The space available will determine the number and size of the buildings to be used, but once the line is laid it is recommended that outlines of the bases of buildings are drawn on to the baseboard. Any compromise necessary on size or siting can then be determined before the buildings are actually constructed. There is nothing more frustrating than finding that a building on which attention has been lavished for several hours does not quite fit in the space intended. It is important that the buildings fit the scene, otherwise the overall effect of the layout is diminished.

Platforms

The principal building is the station, but before this is commenced, it is suggested the platform(s) are put in. Study railway books at the library, and notice the variations found in platform structure. The earlier prototype probably had a straight platform side with large edging bricks. In many cases, the brick wall will have the top few rows, varying from two to as many as five, overhanging the row below, and the edging stones in this case are likely to have been 2×3ft (50×90cm) pieces of stone, or concrete slabs.

As towns get left behind, houses normally show more individuality and thus present opportunities for detailed architectural modelling. This creeper-covered half-timbered house, probably 17th century, shows excellent observation on the part of the builder and is a fine little model in its own right. Modelled by Peter Buddle.

Although platforms are rare in some countries, most European railways have them. Some typical styles are illustrated here, covering virtually a century of railway operation. If a 'period' layout is envisaged, the importance of research cannot be over-emphasised.

A model platform is easily constructed from balsa, with a number of cross-braces to give support to the top which is also made of balsa. Balsa is recommended since it is stiffer and more durable than card, and it comes in a variety of thicknesses. For the platform top a minimum of $\frac{1}{8}$in (3mm) thickness should be used. Once the main platform structure is in place, the brick or stone facings, the edgings and platform surface can be added. Thin balsa or plastic card (styrene sheet) can form the base for the facings, and if rows of overhanging bricks are required, then these are more easily prepared as a separate unit to be fixed when completed. Plastic card will easily score to give stone outlines, or the edges of thickish sheet (1mm in 4mm scale) scored to give single row brick formations.

A study of photographs will enable a platform surface to be selected to suit specific requirements, and in many locations, the platform surface around the station building will have been slabbed or tarmaced, with the outer reaches consisting of loose gravel or deteriorating asphalt. Some very realistic concrete paving slabs are included in the Builder Plus range of model buildings, and the effect of these can be improved if they are scored along the joins lightly with a scriber. One of the simplest ways of achieving a tarmac or fine gravel surface is to use fine grade glass-paper or emery cloth, or the finest grade flour-paper, stuck down with contact adhesive or white PVA; once the glue is dry, it can be coloured to suit requirements with turps-thinned oil paint. Again, refer-

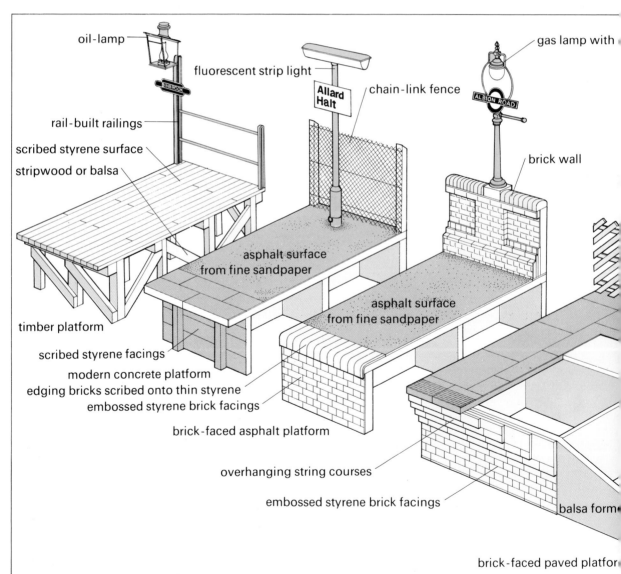

oil-lamp

fluorescent strip light

gas lamp with

rail-built railings

Allard Halt

chain-link fence

ALBION ROAD

scribed styrene surface

stripwood or balsa

brick wall

asphalt surface from fine sandpaper

asphalt surface from fine sandpaper

timber platform

scribed styrene facings

modern concrete platform

edging bricks scribed onto thin styrene

embossed styrene brick facings

brick-faced asphalt platform

overhanging string courses

embossed styrene brick facings

balsa form

brick-faced paved platfor

ence to photographs will give indications of shadings and wear.

Railway buildings

The railway buildings are the most important part of a model railway scene. Most of the buildings in use by British Rail were built by the pre-grouping companies at the time when the early lines were laid, much of this work being done prior to 1900. The railways used good materials, including well-seasoned hardwoods, and it is not surprising that the early buildings survived. In many cases they have remained unaltered right through to the present day. For many modellers, therefore, some research will be necessary if accuracy is to be achieved. Each of the pre-grouping companies had particular characteristics, not

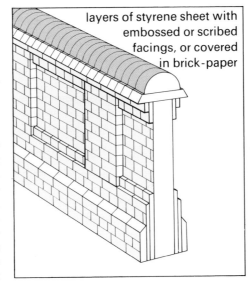

layers of styrene sheet with embossed or scribed facings, or covered in brick-paper

Left: Decorative walls were common features of railway stations in the late 1800s and early 1900s, and many still survive. Fine gravel or asphalt were most often used for platform surfaces; garnet paper can be close to the correct colour for gravel and carborundum paper in the finest grit (below left) represents asphalt well.

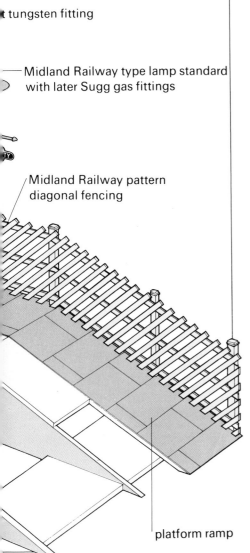

tungsten fitting

Midland Railway type lamp standard with later Sugg gas fittings

Midland Railway pattern diagonal fencing

platform ramp

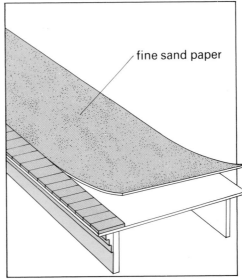

fine sand paper

Below: A typical small country station or 'halt' in the north of England. Photographs of full-size features such as this provide almost all the information needed to make a simple but effective model; dimensions can be approximated by using a known feature such as door height or even rail gauge.

Kits of lineside accessories and buildings abound in most countries. This attractive little signal box comes pre-printed in colour, with moulded accessories which require painting during or after assembly. Weathering techniques should be used to take the newness off the finished result.

only on the types and liveries of locomotives and carriages, but in the building styles which they used; it is important that your railway buildings have identifiable features of the particular company you are representing.

Although the prototype structures lasted for long periods, many have recently been demolished as lines have been closed. Despite this, there are sources which may be able to provide details of a particular location, or more generally of particular types of building. Try the local reference library for photographs and Ordnance Survey maps. Specialist societies like the LNER Study Group, the SR Society, the LMS Society, and others, may be able to assist. Make local enquiries too, for it is just possible that a particular station building is now used for a dwelling or other purpose, and photographs and measurements can then be taken, with permission from the occupier. A railway Rating Plan, showing track layouts and positions of buildings (and from this

approximate ground sizes) will also be of immense assistance.

Stations

There are several commercial ranges of buildings which can be used alongside one another. A most useful one for British modellers is the Prototype range by Slaters, since each model is based on an identified prototype building, and, as an example, the LNWR/LMS Signal Cabin kit can easily be adapted to suit a wide range of particular prototype cabins. Others in the Prototype range can also be altered with the aid of photographs. The model press have carried instructive articles over the years, and it is often possible to obtain back issues of magazines which could provide some of the drawings you require.

Similarly, if a station building from, say, the Superquick or Builder Plus range is used, then once the basic shell of the building is made, detail changes can be made to achieve a model which is different.

With the aid of plastic card, stone facings around windows and doors can be built up and coloured. Many of the early buildings had outside walls several bricks thick, and by adding a thickness of plastic card, or ordinary card on the inside of the model, this effect can be achieved. In most kits the windows are printed on clear acetate sheet. By using thin strips of plastic card the framework of the windows can be built up. For sash windows, the printed window should be cut through and with an additional thickness of card added to form a deeper frame for the lower sash, the sash effect can be achieved. Alterations like this to a basic kit, although time-consuming, can result in a more realistic model which will give greater satisfaction to the modeller, and to those who will later admire the result.

Printed brickpapers can be greatly enhanced by scoring each cement line to give a more realistic brickwork effect. Light pressure with a blunted point, or a well-used craft blade, is sufficient to achieve the desired result, but before embarking on work of this nature, it is best to experiment with a piece of scrap. Other features which lend themselves to easy alteration are fretted barge or facia boards to the gables; drawn out on plastic card and cut with care, they are easily added. Chimneys are another feature and in some of the old railway buildings, the chimneys were of outstanding and ornate design. These again are easily made up from balsa or plastic card and covered with a suitable paper.

Doors on the old buildings were invariably panelled, and here again plastic card can be used to reproduce the true effect, discarding the printed doors in the kit.

There will be a number of windows in a station building and if time has been devoted to altering a kit, or making up a building from scratch, then a little more patience and effort will again bring immense improvement. Interiors can be quickly assembled and coloured to add yet another dimension to the model. With some building kits, printed interiors are provided, and they too can be improved. The pictures on the wall will be better if a fine plastic card frame is added. A table or chair, or in the case of a booking hall, a rail to the booking office window can be added. Include a passenger or two with pieces of luggage, maybe a door ajar, notices on the wall and a clock face.

Many modellers will be satisfied to use the tile printing provided in the kit, or one of the tile sheet designs which are available. However, it is worth remembering that the roof tiles face the modeller and the viewer directly, and they will reflect the available lighting. Any additional work

Nothing looks worse than a door or window perfectly flush with a brick wall. Adding depth to such a structure is not difficult. Treatment for such features is shown here, together with suggestions for making a plain wall a little fancier, in keeping with the style adopted when the buildings were erected.

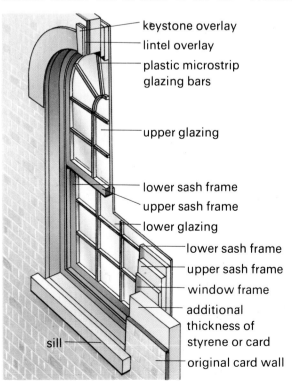

keystone overlay
lintel overlay
plastic microstrip glazing bars
upper glazing
lower sash frame
upper sash frame
lower glazing
lower sash frame
upper sash frame
window frame
additional thickness of styrene or card
original card wall
sill

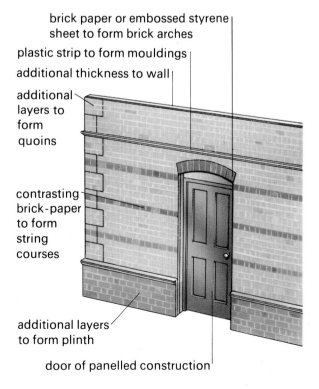

brick paper or embossed styrene sheet to form brick arches
plastic strip to form mouldings
additional thickness to wall
additional layers to form quoins
contrasting brick-paper to form string courses
additional layers to form plinth
door of panelled construction

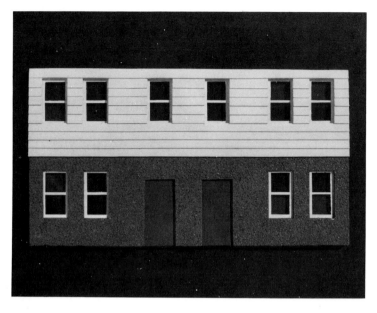

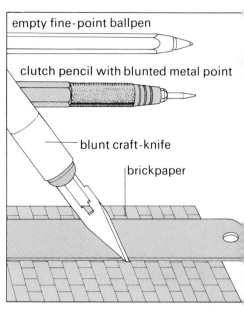

Above left: Complete kits for houses and other buildings are available, but it is also possible to buy component parts. This pair of modern house fronts, with a pebble-dashed base and timber-clad upper storey, can be used for a pair of semi-detached dwellings or as part of a complete terrace.

Above right: Instruments and a method of scoring are shown on the left of this drawing; only light indentations are needed to break up the flat effect given by printed paper or card. For roofs, where strong light falls directly on them, slates or tiles are more effective if laid in rows cut from thin card.

will therefore be more readily noticeable than on vertical surfaces. For this reason, time should be spent on improving the tiling. Plastic card of 10 thou (0.25mm) thickness cut into a strip width which is equal to two tile thicknesses and suitably scored will give a good representation of tiling when laid overlapping to half the thickness, commencing at the lower end of the roof.

It should also be remembered that tiling on many old buildings was carried out by skilled craftsmen, and when thin local stone tiles were used, for example in the Cotswolds, the size of the tiles grew narrower up to the ridge tiles. Sometimes, patterns were included in the tiling. Around the base of chimney stacks lead flashing should be represented, either by painting a medium grey or using very thin plastic card. All these are points which, if used in conjunction with standard station building kits, can result in a model which is representative of the era but also has character and detail. It will not quite be scratch-building, but it is only a short step from it. Scratch technique is briefly as follows.

If the ground dimensions are known for the prototype, and good photographs are available, then rough drawings, if originals are not readily available, can be made up by counting brick courses, for example.

Plastic card, or stiff cardboard if preferred, can be drawn and cut to size, with windows and doorways also cut out. Brickpaper is available in a variety of types and colourings, or for the more experienced modeller, embossed brick plastic card is available, but care with lintels and vertical brick courses is needed. Since modellers continually strive to improve their techniques and standards, an early model, perhaps a small hut, can be used as a test building before embarking on a larger structure.

Another feature common to quite a number of stations throughout Britain and elsewhere was a canopy attached to the station buildings, to provide shelter from the elements for waiting passengers. Some of the building kits do include parts to construct these. One of the main identifying features of canopies was the boarding around the edge. If the kit canopy is to be used, then you can always change the boarding to correspond to a particular type which has been identified from photographs. To construct a canopy from scratch, clear plastic sheet of 20 thou (0.5mm) thickness should be used, and the framework added from ordinary opaque plastic card. When using the clear material take particular care to avoid the cement or solvent flowing too freely and so clouding the transparent glaze. Use a little and repeat if required. If the canopy was a solid structure without glass, then little difficulty should be experienced in using the kit canopy, and merely replacing the outer vertical boards. During construction it is advisable to check the canopy against the station building to ensure a close fit on completion.

Other railway buildings

After the platform and main station build-

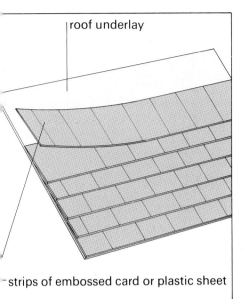

roof underlay

strips of embossed card or plastic sheet

ings you will probably want to include other railway structures. A goods shed, a prefabricated trader's store, a weighbridge hut, and others can be constructed, either from scratch or from the kits readily available. As in the case of the station building, improvements will lead to much more satisfying models.

If the layout is large enough with sufficient traffic to demand one, a locomotive depot can also be featured. However, all too often, modellers try to fit a locomotive depot into too small a space with the result that overcrowding becomes inevitable; this detracts from the overall appearance of the layout. Studying a locomotive shed layout on a track or rating plan will show that the area covered by the prototype location is often considerable. To achieve the right result sufficient space must therefore be allocated. If this is not possible, and a small shed is not appropriate, then the modeller would be well advised to eliminate the locomotive shed requirement from his plans.

Photographs from as many angles as possible are essential, and from these, many points will become apparent. The model locomotive shed is perhaps one type of railway building which is not too well-catered for in British outline kits. However, from photographs it will be seen that most shed doors were open, particularly at busy sheds, and in later days the doors were removed altogether. Interior details are also important: some interior walls were whitewashed, or white glazed bricks were used, and spare lamps, buckets and

shovels, wheelbarrows and many more items were always to be found in and around the shed. Outside would be found the yard lamps and watercranes, a coaling stage or tower, and one feature rarely included in a shed scene, the ash trolleys, which in many cases ran on rails below the level of and in between the main running rails. Spare locomotive boilers and driving wheels were not normally in evidence at the majority of locosheds, but often the railway modeller will mistakenly add them to his scene.

Above: Simple structures are often overlooked when planning a layout, yet what could look nicer than this old timber barn? Model by Peter Buddle, who also built the house below.

Below: The gable end of the period house shown on page 91.

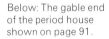

ledge under booking-office window

timetable

clock

bicycle

picture and dado rails

posters

handrail

door fixed in open position

miniature figures

luggage

seats

frame around picture

Above: Not everyone is concerned with interior detail in buildings, but obviously empty shells are unconvincing. The sort of detail that can be included in a booking hall and waiting room is suggested here, and can be emphasised on a dull afternoon or at night by battery-fed interior lighting.

Opposite: Unusual touches add individuality to any layout. The elaborate public clock in this photograph is on a building on the street, but many stations display a clock, or even a turret with four clock faces. With so many miniature watches now inexpensively available, a working clock would not be an impossibility.

All railway buildings should be carefully placed for realism, particularly where one has to compromise in loosely following original rating and track plans. The railway scene also included boundary and platform fencing, walls, barrow crossings made from wooden sleepers, gates, signals and loading gauges, and areas in some goods yards were neglected and overgrown. On the platforms were nameboards, lamp-posts, barrows and trolleys, luggage, milkchurns, and quite frequently pigeon baskets, boxes of day-old chicks, mailbags and heavy items in rough sacking. All these, and many more items, have a part in your railway scene and a study of station photographs will give you an indication of placings.

The nature of one's railway layout will determine whether the buildings are to be permanently fixed in position, located on blocks or slotted between kerbs and steps. The method seen at Pendon Museum is excellent; the structures do not stop at ground level but have their own 'foundations' which go into the base of the scenery, rather than sit prettily but perhaps unevenly upon it. This method, however, is really only suitable on a layout which will be permanently constructed. The buildings are placed in position and the surrounding scenery, roads, fields etc., added around

the base which then becomes submerged. If your layout is to be portable, then you are strongly advised to make all buildings slot into position, so that when movement does take place, they can be removed leaving very little on the boards to be damaged. The platforms are best secured permanently to the baseboards, as this will ensure that these long, thin constructions will not warp. Station buildings can be wedged between the outside steps and the platform, and for those buildings which stand in isolation, a block of wood to fit snugly into the base of the building can be glued to the baseboard.

Tunnels and bridges

Most layouts have, out of sheer necessity, a tunnel at one or both ends and there are several mouldings of tunnel mouths available. As with buildings, photographs will provide the modeller with details of specific tunnel openings to enable a scratch-built feature to be made if necessary. It is also possible to obtain drawings for some tunnel structures. However, seldom do we see a model of a brick ventilation tower protruding from the natural scenery above the path of a tunnel. These were common features from the early railway days and they are still in existence today, although their purpose

was to release thick smoke. The smaller ones had an iron grid on top to prevent mischievous young children from looking too closely, whilst the larger ones were 30–45ft (9–14m) diameter and more than 30ft (9m) high. If you wish to add one to your tunnel start by using the cardboard tube from the inside of a kitchen paper roll. They were also a necessity if a tunnel passed through a town and could be found in between buildings, or on open waste ground.

Bridges were also owned by the railway and again, photographs will give the necessary information on the number of brick courses, the type of stone used, or other structural features. Plastic card is the ideal material to work with, possibly over a balsa framework. Viaducts are somewhat different and there is much more work involved in producing these. No hard and fast rules are given, but a good example of a viaduct made from plastic card is the Millersdale layout. The stone supports have been handcrafted from cast plaster blocks. Each stone shape has been carefully noted from the original and drawn on to the plaster block, then carved out to correspond with photographs of the original. Timber was also used in the construction of some of the early railway viaducts, and one such structure in model form is the Walkham Viaduct, a superb reproduction of an original Brunel viaduct, which has been incorporated into the Dartmoor layout at the Pendon Museum.

American and Continental prototypes

The American and Continental railways have their own particular charms, and

This splendid example of an Edwardian station is typical of many British suburbs. It was designed and constructed by John Piper of Scalelink.

A photograph taken at 'eye level' beneath the station canopy is uncannily lifelike in its attention to structural detail and finish.

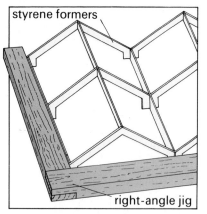

A simple double-pitch canopy built as a unit can easily be extended, both in length or by number of units, to cover any type of building from a single platform to a terminus.

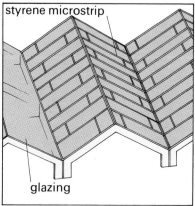

Glazing can be sheets of acetate or clear polystyrene glued to the trusses with styrene microstrip or thin strips cut from veneer glued in place to reproduce the glazing bars.

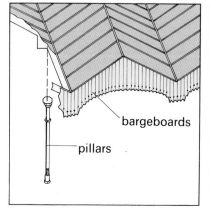

Add the bargeboards, made in reality from vertical lengths of tongue and groove timber, but represented here by scored card. Mount the complete canopy firmly on pillars made from wood dowel and card punchings.

without a personal knowledge of a particular railway then the modeller is dependent on photographs and books. The English railway scene could perhaps be described as largely pastoral, and its familiarity has undoubtedly been responsible for much detail being taken for granted.

With the North American railways, there is the opportunity to model in dramatic contrasts. The lines across the prairie run for long distances quite straight, and with grain stores towering high enough to be seen for miles. Even though this is a simple scene to create, with few buildings which could be said to demand absolutely accurate drawings, the overall vast landscape would provide the problem. However, the mountainous Rockies do lend themselves to recreation

in miniature, but it must be remembered that the sheer height from rail level was much greater than anything encountered in the British Isles. Remember too, that a locomotive and ten wagons, or a push–pull serving a crowded platform, was not the order of the day. If one does seek to model the American or Canadian railways, then either a town station, or a Rockies location offer possibilities. The station buildings were distinctive and often the wooden board construction was painted white.

The Continental scene provides another distinct contrast, and it is easier for the modeller to reproduce a convincing and realistic layout. Again, there is a variety of building kits in moulded plastic and card to provide the basic for individual structures. With attention to detail and care in

Overleaf: An American logging type railroad in H0 gauge which includes a lake crossed by two-level bridgeworks. The lake is made from poured resin and a fisherman in a small boat adds to the water effect.

Below: Cast ironwork was very common at the turn of the century and is often best represented in small scale by etched copper sheet. John Piper built this overbridge, staircase and canopy using fine castings in which he specialises.

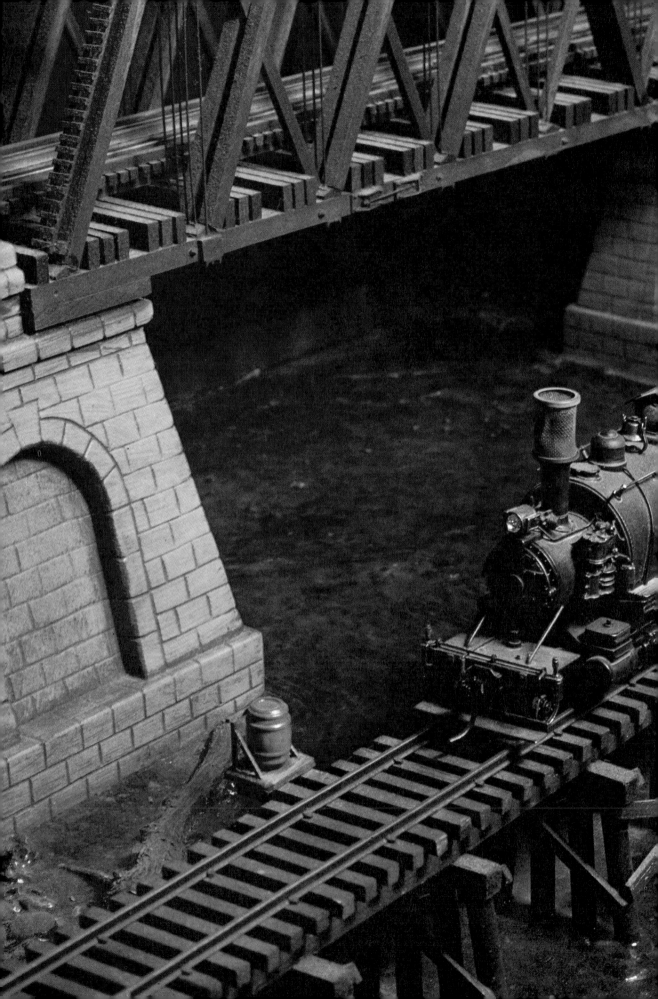

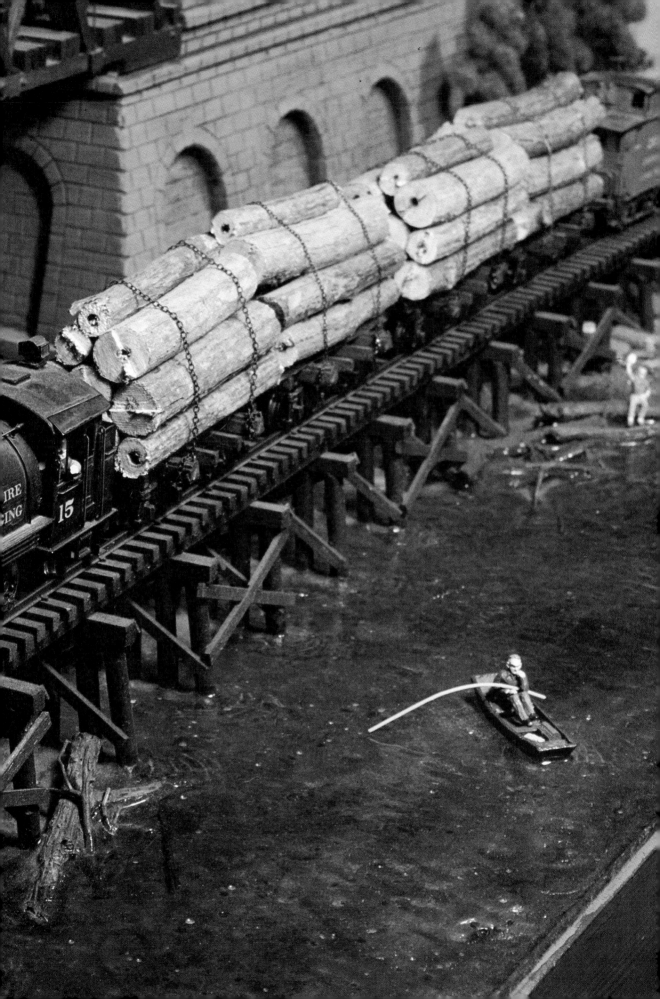

construction, superb models can result. The same detail points for the British scene apply whatever prototype is modelled.

Dwellings and shops

Important though the railway is in the general layout context, it should not be forgotten that non-railway structures also need to be modelled and these can vary widely in type and colouring in most locations.

The nearer to a particular prototype scene modelled, the more accuracy is called for in modelling non-railway buildings. However, if the scene is general, then the modeller has the licence to be able to include models which appeal to him, and not necessarily all from one particular village or town. At Pendon, original thatched cottages have been selected from several villages in the Vale of the White Horse, and the models together make up a representative period village scene. You can do the same to blend your selection of buildings to complete the scene.

The construction techniques already described for the railway buildings also apply to the other buildings you require. It is highly unlikely that original drawings will be available, so photographs and sketches with measurements will assist in making accurate models. It is worth noting such detail as the colour toning of brickwork and signs, particularly where you can still see the prototypes. The building kit ranges include a variety of models both period and modern which are suitable, and it should not be too difficult to change the character and purpose of the basic kits to bring some individuality to your scene.

There are infinite variations possible with chimneys, which tend to strike the observer of a model layout since he is usually looking down on the buildings. For example, there are many different types of pots and cowls, and since some are local products it pays to study the common patterns in any area. Model by John Piper of Scalelink.

One particular kit in the Builder Plus range which lends itself to easy alteration is the small Terrace House. This model is typical of the rows of back-to-back types of dwelling found in towns and cities, many of which were altered to include shop fronts for the butcher, the baker and greengrocer. The first stage is to separate the principal parts and remove window blanks. The ground floor brickwork at the front of two of the houses is then removed and, using plastic card, a replacement front built up whilst the parts are still flat. Small-pane windows can be represented by fine plastic card strips on clear plastic sheet, but in the pre-1939 years many butchers, fruiterers and fishmongers had open shop fronts. It may well be possible to canni-

balise parts from one kit to add to another. The box shape is now formed and completed as required, with either the tiling from the kit, or using one of the other methods previously mentioned. Interior details can be added and an open shop window provides an opportunity to add realistic detailed goods. For the greengrocer, apples and oranges, melons and bananas can be formed by loading a hot soldering iron and lightly throwing the molten solder on to a board or in shallow sand. There are other ways (beads, seeds and pulses among them) but a little paint will provide the finishing touch to whichever method is adopted.

This same small Terrace House kit will also lend itself to low relief adaptation. The kit is printed back and front, and for use in limited spaces, or to form a back scene, the gables can be cut through. This will give two 'fronts' which can be placed side-by-side, or a narrow 'entry' left between the two halves to give access to the rear of the houses. The same attention to windows, lintels, doors, tiles and chimneys as suggested for railway buildings will improve the houses. Models should be weathered to look lived in—study real buildings to see how they really age and discolour.

Perspective effects and accuracy

There are few kits available for perspective modelling and this effect has to be constructed from scratch. The depth of space available behind the railway area on the

A fine terrace of houses with imposing front fence and gateways modelled by John Piper. Always consider the rationale—such houses would be most likely to be built in towns, and then probably not near the railway, so whether to include this sort of dwelling will depend on how extensive your town model is.

layout will determine the severity of perspective modelling. If there is a large area for scenery then a natural perspective will follow with buildings placed further away from the edge of the layout. But if only limited space is left, then perspectives have to be worked out and verticals reduced from normal width, in some cases to a narrow strip. Horizontal features such as window ledges and lintels are similarly reduced and tapered away from the front, and individual bricks which are visible at the front of the model must be shaded to overcome cement lines on the printed brickwork, until the verticals are indiscernible. Pavements and roadways must also taper away to achieve the right effect, whilst the joint between the rear baseboard

edge and the vertical backscene can be overcome by a bend in the street to one side. The buildings on the bend can be obtained by using smaller scale buildings, in the case of a 4mm scale layout, by using buildings from the 2mm scale range. There are endless permutations for achieving the right blend in model railway scenes.

Only you, the modeller, can decide what will be required for the scenes you are planning. Your ideas will be influenced by various factors; perhaps you will wish to recreate a scene you have known in real life. Research work pays rich dividends. Seek out plans and photographs, from official railway sources, from photograph lists, libraries and museums. The more you are able to achieve a likeness to the proto-

Above: Commercial H0 track and hand-built scenic effects combine with a small American country station to form an attractive layout feature, enhanced by the figures used.

Opposite: Commercial shop and house fronts can be used for low-relief models when square on to the viewer. Variety can be introduced by painting or papering adjoining fronts differently.

type, the more satisfying your model railway will become.

Do not overcrowd your boards, plan carefully, and during construction work carefully on the models to achieve accuracy. Remember also that the work of others can be the means of improving your own standards, so take the trouble to visit model museums and exhibitions renowned for their accuracy and high standards.

In closing this chapter, perhaps it should be pointed out that detailed instructions which are a mere repetition of those contained in all good building kits have been deliberately avoided, it being felt better to concentrate on advice and suggestions which will encourage modellers to try to achieve something a little different from the standard models available. In this way, the individuality of the model is increased, together with the pride and pleasure derived from it by the builder.

Artesian wells are commonplace in most countries; this one is built from a kit of parts. These structures are placed above boreholes leading to water deposits, often on a change of ground contour. So you should strictly read up on Artesian wells and subterranean watercourses to make sure you have it sited appropriately!

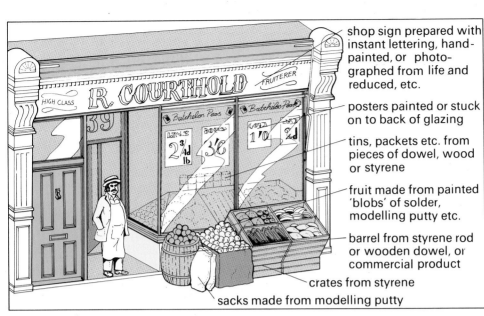

shop sign prepared with instant lettering, hand-painted, or photographed from life and reduced, etc.

posters painted or stuck on to back of glazing

tins, packets etc. from pieces of dowel, wood or styrene

fruit made from painted 'blobs' of solder, modelling putty etc.

barrel from styrene rod or wooden dowel, or commercial product

crates from styrene

sacks made from modelling putty

Shops are fun to model and have a particular attraction for young visitors. That suggested on the left is a fruiterer's.

Clock turrets are featured on some station buildings as well as on stables, when they usually carry a weather vane. The stables might be part of a country mansion complex, or racing stables; either gives opportunities for something a little different.

LOCOMOTIVES

While track and scenery might provide the basic environment, it is the locomotive which adds life to an otherwise passive railway scene and provides the focal point of interest. To set the first train in motion on one's newly-laid track is a rewarding experience, and if the locomotive is scratch-built the reward is much greater.

Today the scope offered to the railway modeller for collecting locomotives is tremen-dous and, in the more popular H0 and 00 scale at least, perhaps bewildering. Three basic approaches are possible, purchasing ready-to-run models, assembling kits and scratch building (definition 'scratch': start from the very beginning or without advantage or preparation, i.e from basic raw materials). Indeed, there are many enthusiasts whose chief interest in the hobby is the construction of model locomotives.

Preceding pages: This unpainted locomotive was built from one of the earliest of the brass kits and is a 2-6-0 of the Wabash line.

Right: One of the most popular and useful British locomotives is the 0-6-0 side tank J72. This Mainline Railways' 00 model is in the old NER livery, but the locomotive is listed in BR black in their catalogue and thus can be used on most British layouts up until about 1960.

Locomotive types

Before looking at models and modelling techniques in more detail it is appropriate to examine first the basics of the prototype; steam, diesel and electric.

Steam locomotives fall into two main categories, tank locomotives and tender locomotives. Tank locomotives would generally be used for the shorter hauls and for shunting or switching. Fuel and water supplies would be carried on the locomotive itself, fuel usually in a bunker behind the cab, and water in tanks either alongside or over the boiler, (hence the terms side and saddle tank). Variations can be found on the basic themes, perhaps the most noteworthy being the Beyer Garratt articulated locomotive which, whilst technically a tank locomotive, was in effect a large boiler slung between two engines upon which were mounted the fuel bunkers and water tanks.

Tender locomotives carried fuel and water supplies in a separate vehicle (tender) coupled to the locomotive and generally had a longer range than the tank locomotive while providing greater stability at high speeds. Some tank locomotives were notoriously unstable due to the surge of water in the tanks.

The number of wheels on a locomotive would be governed by the weight allowed on each axle by the Civil Engineer to give safe passage without damage to track and bridges. The fixed wheel base would be dictated by the radius of track curvature. The weight of the train which would be started from rest by the locomotive would

largely be governed by the 'adhesive weight'. This is the portion of the total locomotive weight actually bearing on the driving wheels (those mechanically coupled to the pistons). Leading and trailing carrying wheels might be used to distribute the weight for a variety of reasons such as track curvature, bridge loading, quality of riding etc; in practice a locomotive with a leading four-wheeled bogie, for example, would ride more steadily and have less tendency to spread the track on curves than a locomotive with only a coupled rigid wheel base.

The Whyte notation, which came into popular use in Britain around the turn of the century, simplified the task of describing locomotive wheel arrangements by first counting the number of leading carrying wheels, then the number of coupled driving wheels and finally the trailing carrying wheels, if any. Thus a locomotive with a leading four-wheeled bogie and four driving wheels but no trailing carrying wheels would be a 4-4-0, while what had previously been referred to as a four-coupled trailing bogie tank engine would be an 0-4-4T. Variations would occur where articulated locomotives were involved—for example, 2-8-8-2 would signify possibly a Beyer Garratt locomotive as used by the LNER, having two engine units each with the wheel arrangement 2-8-0. To complicate matters further, the tendency on mainland Europe was to count the axles, consequently a 4-6-2 in Britain would be referred to as a 2-3-1 in France.

The advent of diesel and electric traction

increased the tendency to count the axles but using letters for the driving axles instead of figures. We therefore have a conventional double-bogie diesel locomotive where all four wheels on each bogie are powered referred to as a Bo-Bo and with six wheel bogies as a Co-Co. On the odd occasions where non-driving carrying wheels are used, figures would represent these axles, for example, 1-Co-Co-1, A1A-A1A.

In the majority of cases type names are used to identify differing wheel arrangements, some of the more popular being Pacific (4-6-2), Mogul (2-6-0), Prairie (2-6-2) and Mikado (2-8-2).

Ready-to run
Returning to model locomotives, it will be apparent that ready-to-run (RTR) locomotives are obvious time-savers and are a boon where the necessary skill has not yet been acquired to build either from a kit or from scratch. Three sources are available, firstly, mass-market good-quality items aimed at the toy market but with the modeller very much in mind; these are very cheap and reliable. Secondly, imported brass models, accurate and well detailed although quite expensive; and finally the professionally-built model, usually extremely accurate and built to order or on short production runs. These are quite often built to the purchaser's own specification and their cost reflects the amount of detail incorporated.

Before the Second World War, and for many years afterwards, the railway modeller had little choice of rolling stock and locomotives and the quality of the available mass-market ready-to-run models was poor. In recent years the market has developed considerably. Amongst the leaders in this field were Rivarossi in the early 1950s with a number of H0 gauge models of Italian prototypes. The British market was beginning to be catered for by Graham Farish, Hornby and Tri-ang with varying degrees of success. Most 00 gauge lines of the period showed at least one example of Tri-ang's LMS 0-6-0 'Jinty' side tank locomotive, a success story which was to be repeated at the end of the decade by its smaller brother in TT gauge. Rivarossi, Fleischmann, Marklin and other mainland European manufacturers produced a vast range of Continental prototypes and were noted for the fine detail and impressive performance when compared with their contemporary British counterparts.

Not until the 1970s did the British mass-market suppliers begin to shake off the 'toy' image. True, some of the Hornby Dublo and Tri-ang models of ten years earlier had been quite interesting when modified and given extra detailing; in fact they are still sought after as subjects for conversion but they were not really fully acceptable as scale models. Now, however, the manufacturers had begun to develop the idea of a mass-produced locomotive robust enough to withstand rough-handling as a toy but correctly proportioned, detailed and finished to sell to the serious enthusiast also. Many modellers would perhaps agree that the 00 gauge

Some companies produce locomotives which are typical of particular purposes rather than scale models of a specific class. Fleischmann describes this one simply as a 'Steam locomotive of a local railway' and it would certainly blend in on a branch line of a Central European layout without attracting curiosity.

Above: One of the
longest H0
locomotives, the Union
Pacific Mallett 'Big
Boy' by Rivarossi.

Right: Still the steam
record-holder, the
Class A4 'Mallard'
available in 00 gauge
from Hornby.

Right: A popular British
subject is this London
Brighton and South
Coast Stroudley Terrier,
from a Thames K kit.

Below: The Bachmann H0 scale Northern GS4 4-8-4 express locomotive in Southern Pacific livery.

Above left: German Class 66 passenger tank locomotive, 2-6-4 notation, in H0 gauge by Piko.

Left: Rivarossi's old-time wood-burner 'J. M. Bowker' of the Virginia and Truckee Railroad.

LNER class J72 0-6-0 tank locomotive, produced in 1976 by Palitoy under the 'Mainline' label, set the standard for the current range of high-quality plastic-bodied units, in much the same way as the Tri-ang 'Jinty' had revolutionised the market 20 years earlier.

Where the accent is on operation or the creation of a large layout with a multiplicity of locomotives and rolling stock, the modeller must decide whether or not he has the time or the skill to hand-build or kit-build the locomotives. He may decide that the time and money available would be better spent creating the overall layout. The range of cheap, well-detailed and commendably accurate ready-to-run locomotives from Airfix, Hornby, Lima, Palitoy (Mainline) and Wrenn, to name the British suppliers, is such that a reasonably representative collection may be built up at a relatively small outlay and provide locomotives which would not disgrace the finest scenic layout and would satisfy all but the most pedantic of enthusiasts.

A survey of types currently available at the time of going to press or about to be released, is given below. In addition to this some of the earlier types may still be found on the second hand market, for example, the Tri-ang L1 4-4-0 and M7 0-4-4T, but these would not of course be comparable in detail and finish to the latest examples.

Great Western Railway prototypes
Mainline Collett 2251 Class 0-6-0
Mainline Manor Class 4-6-0
Hornby King Class 4-6-0
Hornby Hall Class 4-6-0
Hornby 57xx Class 0-6-0 Pannier Tank
Hornby 2721 Class 0-6-0 Pannier Tank
Hornby 0-4-0 No. 101
Lima King Class 4-6-0
Lima 94xx Class 0-6-0 Pannier Tank
Lima 45xx Class 2-6-2 Tank
Lima AEC Railcar
Wrenn Castle Class 4-6-0
Airfix Castle Class 4-6-0
Airfix 14xx Class 0-4-2 Tank
Airfix 61xx Class 2-6-2 Tank

Southern Railway prototypes
Wrenn West Country Class 4-6-2
Wrenn R1 Class 0-6-0 Tank
Hornby E2 Class 0-6-0 Tank
Hornby King Arthur Class 4-6-0

Tiny N gauge locomotive by Lima— the coin is about 30mm at its widest point. This Shay-type engine, unusual for the use of vertical cylinders, would burn most fuels and was widely used in North American logging and surface mining operations. Note the distinctive drive mechanism.

LMS prototypes
Mainline rebuilt Patriot 4-6-0
Mainline Jubilee 4-6-0
Wrenn Duchess 4-6-2
Wrenn City 4-6-2
Hornby unrebuilt Patriot 4-6-0
Hornby Class 5 4-6-0
Hornby Duchess 4-6-2
Hornby 'Jinty' 0-6-0 Tank
Hornby Fowler 2-6-4 Tank
Airfix 4F 0-6-0
Airfix rebuilt Royal Scot 4-6-0
Mainline rebuilt Royal Scot 4-6-0
Mainline 'Crab' 2-6-0

LNER prototypes
Mainline J72 0-6-0 Tank
Hornby Flying Scotsman 4-6-2
Hornby B12 4-6-0
Hornby Mallard 4-6-2
Hornby Sandringham 4-6-0
Hornby J83 0-6-0 Tank
Wrenn A4 Streamlined 4-6-2
Hornby V2 2-6-2

British Railways prototypes (steam)
Mainline Standard Class 4 4-6-0
Wrenn Standard Class 4 2-6-4T

Hornby Britannia 4-6-2
Hornby Standard Class 9 2-10-0
Hornby Standard Class 2 2-6-0

British Railways prototypes (diesel)
Hornby Classes 08, 25, 29, 35, 37, 47, 52
    High Speed Train, Advanced Passenger
    Train
Mainline Class 45 'Peak' and Warship
Airfix Brush A1A-A1A
Lima Warship, Western, Deltic, Class 33,
    Class 09
Wrenn Class 08, Class 20

After considering aspects of appearance and scale proportions, perhaps the biggest problem with the early ready-to-run models was the discrepancies in the wheel standards. This meant that they only operated satisfactorily on track produced by the maker of the locomotive, a throwback to the toy 'train set' approach. Current models have largely overcome this and will usually perform without problems on commercial and hand-built track laid to normal 00 gauge standards, though not on EM, Scalefour and similar layouts without considerable modification.

A question of scale
Reference to EM and other standards leads to the scale/gauge ratio and the different approaches to locomotives and to modelling in mainland Europe and North America. Whilst British models of this size are universally built to a scale of 4mm : 1ft and usually run on 16.5mm gauge track (00 gauge), European and American models scale $3\frac{1}{2}$mm : 1ft (H0 scale) but also run on 16.5mm gauge track. Remembering that the prototype track gauge is 4ft $8\frac{1}{2}$in it will be obvious that the H0 scale produces the more accurate scale/gauge ratio, hence the emergence in Britain of EM (18mm) gauge, Scalefour and similar more accurate scales, although these do not come in the ready-to-run category.

The full-size British locomotive is smaller in height and width than its Continental or Trans-Atlantic counterpart and it is a happy coincidence that a 4mm scale British locomotive would consequently not look out of place alongside, say, a German or Canadian model. These last two would, in turn, be able to negotiate the rather restricted model British tunnels and bridges. For those modelling the North American scene the number of mass-market ready-to-run locomotives is sur-

Above: An H0 model of a Deutsche Bundesbahn Class 144 multi-purpose locomotive by Roco.

Right: A French INOX Z5100 suburban railcar in H0 scale by leading French makers Jouef.

Left: Heavy mountain service Class 1020 electric locomotive of the Austrian railways by Kleinbahn, of Austria.

Below: Another German electric locomotive, Fleischmann's H0 gauge express Class 103. Fleischmann was founded in 1887.

prisingly small. Most emphasis is placed on the more expensive brass RTR or on imports of cheaper models from Europe. Notable exceptions here are the firms of Athearn, specialising in diesels, a typical example being the SD45 six axle 3,600 h.p. hood unit in which all axles are driven, and Mantua, with a range of inexpensive units including a 4-6-4 Hudson, 2-8-4 Berkshire, 2-10-2 Decapod and several switchers. AHM also produce a slightly more expensive range of steam locomotives of which a good example is the 2-8-8-0 Baltimore and Ohio Mallett.

On the imported front, Rivarossi have a very comprehensive selection ranging from the Union Pacific 4-8-8-4 'Big Boy', Norfolk and Western 2-8-8-4 and Union Pacific 4-6-6-4 'Challenger' down to the Baltimore and Ohio 0-4-0 switcher. European ready-to-run models are legion, as will be realised from a glance through the

catalogues of Marklin, Bemo, Fleischmann, Liliput, Lima, Rivarossi, Roco and others. The quality is almost consistently superb and it would be invidious and pointless to single out any particular example on this score alone. Singularly pleasing is the Jouef SNCF 4-8-2 with its attractive green and black livery with red lining whilst the Liliput DB BR18 Pacific is unique as a commercial product because the inside connecting rods are also modelled.

Whilst the 00/H0 scales are the most popular and are well covered by the manufacturers, there is an increasing supply of models for the smaller N gauge or 2mm : 1ft scale with a track gauge of 9mm. Here the anomaly of two scales for one gauge has not been repeated and models of British prototypes look tiny alongside Continental examples. A wide range of Continental N gauge locomotives is avail-

able from Roco, Fleischmann, Arnold, Minitrix and Rivarossi whilst the last named cover a number of North American types including a magnificent Union Pacific 'Big Boy'. British ready-to-run locomotives are available from Graham Farish, Lima and Minitrix and cover such prototypes as British Railways standard 9F 2-10-0, Great Western 'Hall' and LMS Class 5.

The even smaller Z gauge is catered for by Marklin Mini Club whilst TT gauge (3mm : 1ft scale) and 0 gauge (7mm : 1ft scale in Europe, $\frac{1}{4}$in : 1ft scale in North America) modellers must resort to kit or scratch building unless second hand Tri-ang TT equipment can be found, or one is prepared to modify Lima and Atlas 0 gauge models. The choice of spending time running or building is a matter for the individual and must influence initial choice of gauge.

Custom-built and limited-edition models

At the other extreme of the ready-to-run spectrum come the professionally built-to-order locomotives. A number of skilled craftsmen specialise in the production of locomotives where the only limitation on choice of prototype, scale, quality of finish and fineness of detail is the price. The majority of these craftsmen work individually and do not usually advertise, as their production is specialised and limited; perhaps producing as few as fifty or so models in a year. Their commissions are usually obtained by reputation or personal recommendation.

Coming between these two extremes is the limited run 'RTR Brass' market. Generally of Far Eastern origin (for example Japan and South Korea), these are high-quality hand-built locomotives sold through distributors like Pacific Fast Mail with their outlets VH Models in

A powerful electric locomotive is the 'Krokodil' Class Be6/8111 of the SBB (Schweizerische Bundesbahnen) here modelled in H0 gauge by Märklin, a German firm founded in 1859 and a pioneer in most aspects of model railways. These imposing freight locomotives were actually introduced in 1926/7.

Right: Two liveries for
the H0 Plymouth type
diesel switcher by
Bachmann, left Santa
Fe and, right,
Burlington Route.

Below: The sleek
General Motors
'Aerotrain', a different-
looking locomotive,
from a Varney H0 kit.

Right: East German
high-speed railcar, type
VT137, is two-coach,
central bogie driven.
H0 by Piko.

Left: A diesel hydraulic Class 218 German express locomotive in H0 by Lima, an Italian company with an enormous range.

Left: Another Lima model, the American Alco 420, available in four lines' colours or, as shown, U.S. Bicentennial decoration.

Below: A class 118 diesel, by Piko, of the Deutsche Reichsbahn or East German State Railways.

Canada, Fulgurex in Switzerland and Micro Metalsmiths in England. These impressive models are equally suitable as static collectors' items in the original lacquered-brass finish or as reliable runners, painted or unpainted; the variety is tremendous. Naturally, North American prototypes are in the majority, from large mainliners like the United States Railroad Administration standard 2-8-8-2 to some of the quaintest and most exotic old-time Shay and Climax geared locomotives which formerly operated the backwoods logging lines. Recently, a limited number of 4mm scale British outline models have appeared, notably a series of Great Western types including 'King' 4-6-0, 45xx small Prairie 2-6-2T and an 0-6-0 pannier tank in three different versions. The pannier tank in particular is excellent, with full brake gear, enclosed gearbox and motor and plunger type pickups. An 0 gauge version is also available.

Modification of ready-to-run models

The first step towards individuality, and useful as a prelude to kit and scratch building, is the modification of mass-market ready-to-run models. The degree of modification possible, or desirable, depends on the quality of the original, the choice of prototype and the skill of the individual. Choice of prototype is complex. This is where the British approach is likely to be different from that of the European mainlander or those across the Atlantic. British main-line railway companies usually built their own locomotives to designs produced in their own workshops and on the occasions where contracts were put out to private builders, the railway companies' drawings were used. Consequently, the locomotives of each railway had a family resemblance which was unique; a Great Western locomotive, for example, would always be a Great Western locomotive and no amount of modification would disguise the fact. The type could be altered, for example a 'Castle' could become a 'Saint', but the railway company could not be changed.

In contrast, the railways of other countries purchased locomotives from private builders such as Baldwin, Lima and Schenectady in the States, Schneider in France and Henschel, Krupp, Hanomag, Borsig and others in Germany. These builders, like North British, Vulcan,

A Deutsche Bundesbahn Class 050 heavy freight locomotive with a cab tender by Märklin, capable of modification to other classes. The German firm of Merker & Fischer market a conversion set to turn this model into Class 053 as well as conversions for a number of other leading manufacturers' locomotives.

Robert Stephenson in Britain, produced locomotives again with a strong family likeness. The difference was that while the British private builders' designs were mainly for export, the others designed and built for their own country's main lines and consequently virtually identical locomotives could be seen operating with different railway companies. This practice is particularly marked today when, for example, the General Motors Electro Motive Division type GP38 2,000 h.p. road switcher needs little more than a lick of paint or a change of decals to produce examples from Penn Central, CP Rail, Conrail, or Missouri Pacific, while modification to the cab provides a Canadian National variation and an altered short hood would suffice for Norfolk and Western and National Railways of Mexico.

Modifications can range from simply shortening the connection between locomotive and tender (a wide gap is necessary to negotiate the sharp curves in boxed train sets) to the provision of a new chassis under the existing body or perhaps even a new body on the commercial chassis. Between these extremes there is an infinite variety of changes which can be made. Either the appearance can be improved whilst still retaining the original identity, or the locomotive can be converted to another variant of the same type or to a different type altogether.

A coat of matt varnish and the painting out of bright work on the wheels of some models can eradicate the plastic appearance. Further improvement can be made by the careful removal with file or knife of the moulded handrails and replacement by wire.

Some models lend themselves to a variety of identity changes. The Lima 4575 class GWR 2-6-2T with high sloping tanks can be converted to the earlier 4500 type with flat top tanks, whilst the Wrenn (formerly Hornby) Southern Railway rebuilt 'West Country' class Pacific is capable of a number of minor modifications to the tender to give different varieties of the 'West Country' and 'Battle of Britain' classes, whilst more drastic surgery (including lengthening the body by 5mm and fitting larger wheels) can produce its larger brother, the 'Merchant Navy' class. The Hornby LNER B12 4-6-0 can, by the same token, become a B17, 01

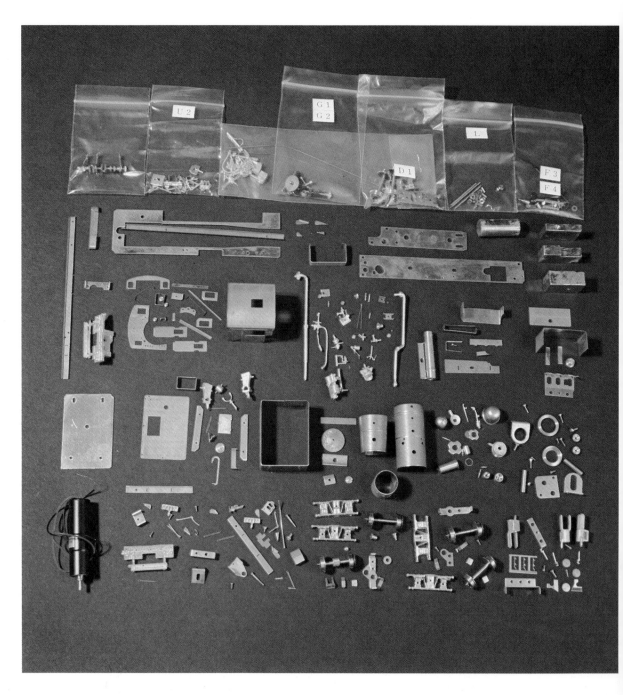

The selection of parts confronting the purchaser of one of the Japanese brass locomotive kits. This is for a 00 model of a 70-ton Shay and is part cast, part stamped; the main crankshaft can be seen in the top left packet. Note that a motor is supplied for builders who want to run the completed model.

2-8-0, D16 4-4-0 and even an ex Great Northern 4-4-2 Atlantic.

Fleischmann produce a German class 50 2-10-0, a class of freight locomotives which totalled 3,171 units built from 1938 onwards. Not surprisingly, a number of variations existed, involving tenders, tender cabs, smoke deflectors etc., and conversion items are available from Merker and Fischer and from Gunther. In the USA Cary Locomotive Works produce a range of boiler and cab conversion units to fit Mantua chassis, including USRA Pacific

4-6-2 and Mikado 2-8-2 types, also diesel bodies and a wide range of lost wax brass parts. Conversion of British 4mm scale 16.5mm gauge locomotives to Scalefour or 18mm gauge can be undertaken, but this is more often the province of the experienced kit or scratch builder and not to be recommended for the beginner.

Kit building

Kit building can take many forms and involve a variety of materials and constructional methods. Again the approach

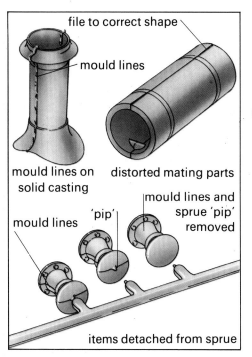

file to correct shape

mould lines

mould lines on solid casting

distorted mating parts

mould lines

'pip'

mould lines and sprue 'pip' removed

items detached from sprue

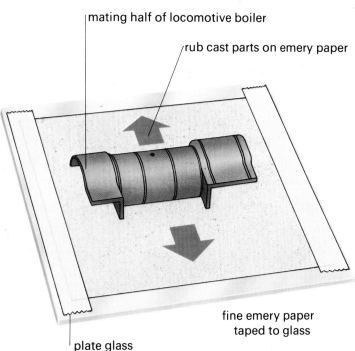

mating half of locomotive boiler

rub cast parts on emery paper

fine emery paper taped to glass

plate glass

is different on opposite sides of the Atlantic. North American practice can be typified by the Bowser Union Pacific Challenger 4-6-6-4 kit which is almost entirely screwed together, being virtually a ready-to-run model in completely 'knocked-down' condition. Mainland European kits are virtually non-existent—it is with the British prototype that a variety can be found.

British kits can be found in four materials, plastic, cast white metal, etched or precut brass and precut nickel silver. Plastic kits were originally introduced as non-motorised static items almost thirty years ago and required nothing more than polystyrene cement for assembly and careful painting to produce an attractive model. Not surprisingly, they quickly became subjects for enterprising scratch builders to motorise by producing a new metal chassis, and one or two conversion kits came on the market. A good example is the Airfix 'Battle of Britain' locomotive which produces an excellent model when combined with a Bristol Models brass chassis kit, Hamblings wheels, an Airfix 5 pole motor and a set of Romford 30:1 gears.

The 1957 Exhibition of the Model Railway Club at Central Hall, London saw the introduction of a cast white metal kit for a 4mm scale 14xx 0-4-2T by K's of Shepherd's Bush. Complete with chassis, motor and wheels, it could be assembled in

under two hours using glue, a modelling knife, small files, screwdriver and a $\frac{1}{8}$in reamer for the axle holes. This modest beginning heralded a complete revolution in model locomotive building. Slowly at first, but with ever increasing momentum, new kits appeared until a recent random check through just one month's issue of a well-known model railway magazine disclosed advertisements for over 150 different kits from ten manufacturers.

By careful selection it is possible to build up a representative stock of locomotives for all regions of British Railways, for the 'Big Four' main lines prior to nationalisation and for many of the old pre 1923 grouping companies. Gem, for example, have extensively covered the London and North Western and North British companies, DJH and others provide a variety of other Scottish examples, while K's and Wills have a wide variety to suit all tastes.

The amount of time and skill required to assemble a cast metal kit varies according to the complexity of the prototype. Simplest of all are the 'Bodyline' type designed, as their name suggests, to provide only the body to fit on to a commercial chassis. Some include cast or etched chassis components, while a relatively small proportion are complete with motor and wheels. A recent innovation is the introduction, in certain kits, of etched brass components where thinner metal gives a decidedly improved visual scale

Moulding flash is inevitable, as on the chimney and buffers shown; often the neatest way to remove it is by scraping with a sharp blade held at right-angles to the mould line. Where warping has occurred, rubbing on fine abrasive paper taped to plate glass or a similar dead flat surface is recommended.

Near right and centre show 'before and after' dealing with flash on a white metal tender. Care must be taken not to scrape or file down rivet detail. Far right shows the underside of the same tender with the bogie trucks fitted.

The locomotive boiler cleaned up and with much of the detail added, near right, and, centre, the chassis complete with smokebox saddle, motion plate etc. but still lacking motion and motor. Far right shows a trial mating of main components.

Near right, the motor, connecting rods and valve gear in place on the chassis; note the worm drive, which does not permit coasting. Centre, close-up of the motion-work on the completed engine and, far right, the whole locomotive and tender.

 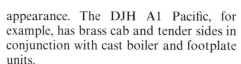 

appearance. The DJH A1 Pacific, for example, has brass cab and tender sides in conjunction with cast boiler and footplate units.

Before starting work on your kit, study all the parts and examine every item of instruction which the manufacturer provides. Then have a dry run, as far as is possible, without any fixing medium, to familiarise oneself with the assembly procedure and to check the fitting of mating components.

The quality, accuracy and cleanliness of modern castings is excellent but nevertheless a certain amount of 'flash' must be removed. This can be carefully achieved by scraping with a sharp knife or by using small files and emery boards. Be careful, as the rivet and other detail is easy to deface but virtually impossible to replace. Any mating parts that are not a perfect fit should be filed and scraped. This is particularly important where two halves of a

boiler come together, and on the seating of the chimney and dome. If difficulty is experienced in obtaining a flat straight edge, for example on the boiler halves or where the tank sides sit down on the footplate, it is worth placing a sheet of fine emery or glasspaper on a truly flat surface and carefully rubbing the component to and fro. A very gentle brushing of the components using a soft wire brush (the type used for cleaning suede shoes) will remove the smaller items of flash and generally tone down the harshness of the castings.

A number of experienced modellers still recommend the use of low-melt solder in the construction of cast-metal kits. Undoubtedly this is the most durable method of assembly but it should be approached with caution as considerable skill is required. However, several adhesives are available and the actual choice is very much a matter of individual taste. Five

class of locomotive. The spare components are useful to keep for future models, either as an aid to scratch building or for further kit modification. Custom modifications may be carried out using Plastic Padding, or similar car filler paste which is easy to carve and file for such items as Belpaire fireboxes and smoke box saddles. Styrene sheet can be used in a similar manner.

Scratch-building

Whilst the true definition of scratch-building implies that the modeller makes everything himself (a few dedicated enthusiasts do just that), it is up to the individual himself to decide what he can make and which components he can buy to match the amount of time, skill and money available. The importance of research cannot be overemphasised. While it is essential to have some knowledge, even when converting commercial models and assembling kits, a full knowledge of the prototype is vital before commencing to scratch-build a locomotive. No matter how careful you think you have been, some self-styled expert will always appear to say 'number 2577 never had a corridor tender' or '60131 should have a flush-sided cab without rivets'.

Obtain a good scale drawing. The various magazines are an excellent source but check that they *are* to the scale indicated as quite often shrinkage or distortion takes place in the printing process. Decide which individual locomotive in a particular class you are going to model and obtain as many photographs as possible from all angles. Check that the photographs are all from the same period, as modifications took place from time to time, and establish that the condition you are modelling the locomotive in coincides with the livery in which you are intending to paint it. Preserved locomotives are notoriously unreliable for confirmation of these points.

It is presumed that the basic tools are already familiar to the reader; obviously if you have a comprehensive tool kit you have fewer finished components to purchase. A lathe is not essential but is useful. A soldering iron (25 watt for general use, larger 65 watt for very heavy jobs, particularly in 0 gauge) and jeweller's piercing saw are essential, as are a number of small files, hand or electric drill and small pliers. A supply of cored solder and a non-acid flux are necessary.

minute epoxy resins (Devcon, Britfix, Araldite, Rapid etc.) offer the ability to adjust the parts slightly before setting hard, but should be used sparingly to avoid a 'glue sandwich' effect, while perhaps the latest cyanocrylate instant adhesives are the most attractive. Gloy Cyano, Holts Superfast, and Loctite Super Glue 3 or equivalents are easily obtainable at motorists' and hardware stores. Loctite 1S 495 industrial adhesive is exceptionally powerful. These adhesives should be handled carefully, they operate by capillary attraction and excess adhesive will run along the joint and could quite easily bond unwanted items, including fingers, to the model. Skin and eye contact *must* be avoided at all times and the working area must be adequately ventilated. Above all, keep adhesives away from children.

A number of kits contain duplicate parts in order that the final model may represent one of a number of variants of the same

The completed model, from an American Bowser kit of an E6 Atlantic locomotive of the Pennsylvania Railroad. These mainly die-cast kits result in quite heavy models which, with suitable gear reduction from the motors, produce excellent running characteristics.

Having selected a good, simple prototype, start with the chassis. A short cut where available would be to use a commercial etched brass kit such as Wills or Kemilway, but this is cheating unless used to gain experience for next time! There are two schools of thought on chassis construction. The first and easiest is to use $\frac{1}{16}$in (1.5mm) thick brass strip with tubular spacers and in this case the use of separate bushes for the axle holes in 4mm scale can be avoided as the frame thickness provides sufficient bearing surface. Secondly, and more prototypically, we can use thin brass, say $\frac{1}{32}$in (0.8mm) and use fabricated stretchers. This method requires less physical effort in cutting out the components and is less likely to produce misalignment of the axle holes due to faulty drilling. In all cases *both* coupling rods and *both* side frames should be secured together and drilled through using a drill of clearance size for the crankpins. Holes for the axle bushes should then be opened out and bushes secured by Loctite rather than soldering.

A wide variety of motors is available, some with gearboxes which are simplicity itself to install, the majority without gearboxes and requiring careful alignment of

worm and gear wheel. Choice depends to a large extent on the size of prototype. The ECM range and Anchoridge D11 and D13 types will fit the smallest British prototypes. Romford and K's are typical British suppliers whilst Japanese KTM (small DH105, large DH13) are also useful. Where the increased cost can be justified the cylindrical coreless 'can' motors by Portescap, Sagami and Canon are exceptionally quiet, smooth and powerful. Gears can be obtained from Millholme, Mikes Models, Ultrascale and others. Useful ratios are 40 : 1 and 50 : 1.

It is now almost universal to adopt the two rail method of current collection, where current is picked up by the wheels on one side and returned via the other side. This means that the wheels on one side of the locomotive must be insulated from the remainder of the chassis. This is variously done by interposing insulation medium between the rim and wheel centre or by using a plastic wheel centre or boss. A third and cheap method would be to cut through each alternate spoke and fill the gap with epoxy resin and then repeat the procedure with the remaining spokes when the first application of resin has set.

Pickups may be spring wire bearing on

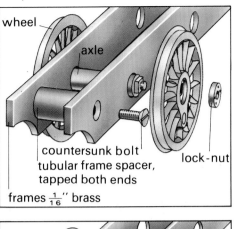

Stiff side-frames held squarely to each other with accurate spacers or stretchers are a basic requirement for trouble-free running.

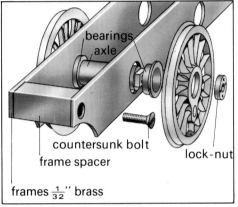

Axles can run in reamed holes in thick frames but need bushes (bearings) when thin frames are used. Note the different form of spacer.

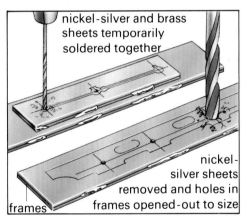

Soldering coupling rods to the frames and drilling all four thicknesses together helps accurate alignment and smooth operation, provided the wheels are accurate.

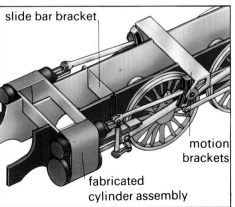

The valve gear is an essential visual part of a steam-outline locomotive but contributes nothing practical. Take care to avoid any friction or binding in it.

the wheel rims, or may be spring plungers bearing on the inside of the rims. Where wheels with plastic centres are used throughout it would be necessary to have pickups on both sides. On tender locomotives rubbing pickups can be avoided by having insulated wheels on one side of the locomotive and on the opposite side of the tender, but it is then necessary to have an insulated drawbar between locomotive and tender.

Transferring dimensions from the drawing to the material for superstructure construction can be a time-consuming exercise, and a system evolved by Mike Edge is useful if a little unorthodox. The components are picked up full size on tracing paper, each piece of tracing paper carrying parts for the same thickness of metal, 0.010 (0.25mm) brass for boiler and any other parts requiring rolling, 0.010 (0.25mm) nickel silver for remaining body parts and 0.020 (0.5mm) brass for frames and coupling rods. The tracings are then affixed to the metal using double-sided adhesive tape and the components cut out using the piercing saw with a very fine blade (Eclipse M4/0 or M3/0). Tin snips tend to distort the metal.

Representation of rivets can be obtained

Right: The parts of a typical electric motor as used in a majority of 00 and H0 locomotives. The main parts to wear are the commutator and the brushes.

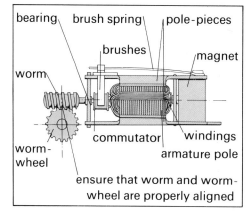

bearing brush spring pole-pieces
brushes
magnet
worm
windings
worm-wheel
commutator
armature pole
ensure that worm and worm-wheel are properly aligned

Right: Solid axles with two-rail pick-up mean that the wheels must be insulated from the axles and wipers used on the wheels to transmit the collected current.

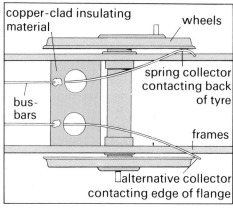

copper-clad insulating material wheels
spring collector contacting back of tyre
bus-bars
frames
alternative collector contacting edge of flange

Right: Methods of separating the positive and negative electrical flows include insulating both wheels, one wheel only, or splitting the axles as drawn.

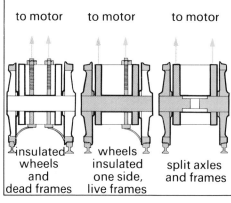

to motor   to motor   to motor
insulated wheels and dead frames
wheels insulated one side, live frames
split axles and frames

Right: An alternative method is to use one set of locomotive wheels and the opposite set of tender wheels to collect and return the current to the rails.

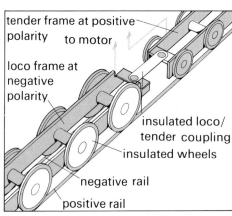

tender frame at positive polarity
to motor
loco frame at negative polarity
insulated loco/tender coupling
insulated wheels
negative rail
positive rail

1

2

3

4

5

too thin too thick correct

with a centre punch, with a lead block used as an anvil, if a commercial riveting tool is not available. The etched brass kits mentioned earlier provide the builder with components which effectively bypass the onerous, time-consuming tasks of marking out and cutting, enabling all one's efforts to be concentrated on assembly and fitting. Rivets and other details, for example, window frames, beading etc., are usually produced in relief and enable an extremely fine model to be produced.

On a British prototype, assembly would commence with the footplate. American locomotives were notably short on this useful part of the anatomy and here it is necessary to start with the boiler on which everything else is hung. Hence the reference earlier to the Carey Locomotive Works boiler and cab conversion units.

At all times it is essential to maintain squareness of assembly and wherever possible soldering should be done from the inside to minimise (or avoid altogether) the need to clean up afterwards. An excellent policy is to build up sub-assemblies, e.g. footplate with edge angles and buffer beams, cab tanks and bunker, boiler and smokebox etc., and to screw these together.

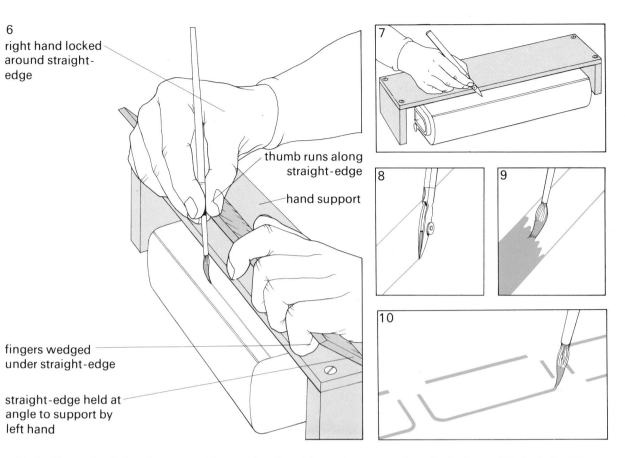

6
right hand locked around straight-edge

thumb runs along straight-edge

hand support

fingers wedged under straight-edge

straight-edge held at angle to support by left hand

This facilitates final cleaning up and is an aid to painting, particularly where two or more colours are involved.

Painting

The application of paint can improve a mediocre model or can ruin an excellent model, depending on the skill of the painter. It is best left to experts unless one has use of an airbrush and knows how to handle it. Lining is another tricky operation and is best carried out using a draughtsman's ruling pen. Preparation for painting, however, is within anyone's capabilities if care is taken. Avoid highly-polished metal surfaces, otherwise the primer will not 'key' and the paint will flake. All grease and solder flux etc. must be removed by immersing in warm water containing soap powder or mild detergent and gently rubbing with a small ($\frac{1}{4}$–$\frac{1}{2}$in) (6–12mm) paintbrush. Watch the temperature of the water; soldered components will withstand anything you can bear your hands in, but some of the adhesives can break down at even relatively low temperatures. Rinse off with clean water and dry carefully (cotton wool buds as sold in baby shops can be handy

here) and leave in a warm (not hot) place to dry off completely.

Aerosol cans of paint for spraying car bodies are useful as primers where a suitable colour exists. Matt black applied in a warm atmosphere assumes a much more acceptable satin sheen than if its gloss counterpart was used. Some car body paint colours do approximate to railway liveries. For example, British Leyland Damson doubles nicely for LMS red. Check the shade cards at your local garage but be prepared for a disappointment—no one yet seems to have a Great Western green.

In search of knowledge

One chapter can only touch on the very wide subject of locomotives. For those wishing to become deeply involved, many specialist volumes have been written. The monthly magazines on both sides of the Atlantic provide details of new products, new methods, hints on operation and many other aspects and are invaluable. Membership of the local Model Railway Club provides a means of exchanging views and talents and is to be strongly advised.

Painting is the skill which most often eludes modellers, and certainly achieving a neat and clean result on a tiny model is taxing. Experiment and practice are the only answers, but the tips illustrated here may help. Take trouble to get the paint to the right consistency, keep the pens and brushes absolutely clean and you're half way!

ROLLING STOCK

For many people, the first step from that initial circle of track to lasting enjoyment of the hobby is the recognition that railways embrace more than the *Queen of Scots* or the *Orient Express*. Furthermore, real trains do not chase their tails, they go from A to B carrying people and commodities with a purpose. Immediately, you face a problem: you may not appear to have room for more than one station, although an L-shape occupying two walls of a room has been feasible for many people with limited space, with a station at one end of the L and either a station or hidden sidings (staging tracks) at the other. But even if a circle has to be accepted (and it does have some advantages), the illusion of going somewhere is enhanced if part of the track is out of sight. Operation becomes the key-note instead of tail-chasing. It is interesting to note that many of the most successful and long-lasting layouts were designed chiefly with operation in mind.

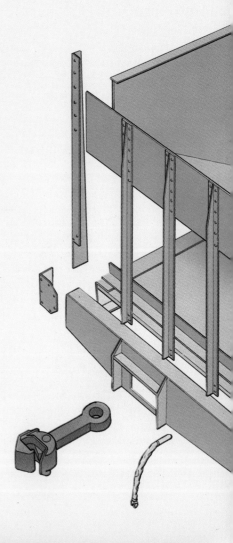

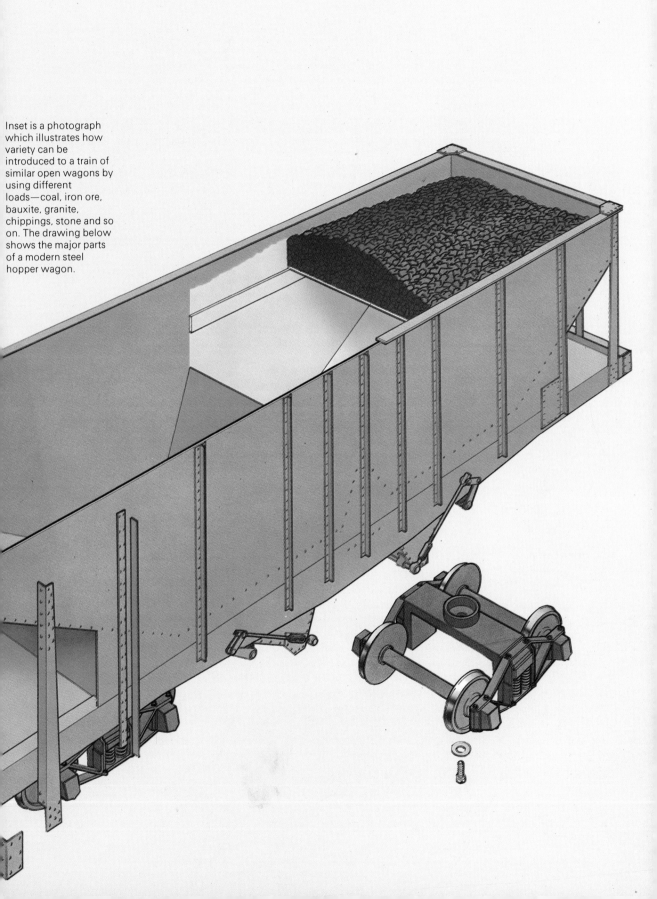

Inset is a photograph
which illustrates how
variety can be
introduced to a train of
similar open wagons by
using different
loads—coal, iron ore,
bauxite, granite,
chippings, stone and so
on. The drawing below
shows the major parts
of a modern steel
hopper wagon.

Giving your layout a theme

You should now review the vehicles you have acquired: are they suitable for the traffic? Those countries with substantial passenger services obtain and assign their vehicles in three ways: purpose-building, cascading down, and (less frequently) re-building. What you might expect to find, therefore, are a rake of modern main line coaches on principal schedules; an older generation of main line coaches on medium and long distance secondary services; recent suburban stock for the more important local trains; and worn-out relics ambling towards retirement on the lowliest duties, or being retained solely for rush-hour traffic. Rebuilding stock may give it a new lease of life for revenue service, but it also provides vehicles for maintenance and repair trains (and even trains for erecting electric catenary).

Accommodation also varies. Local trains need few 1st class seats, but a much greater demand is evident on long distance services, so balance your stock accordingly. En route, some trains are split to serve different destinations, and should be marshalled to assist this. Any segment may be one coach or several; British Rail's corridor brake composite, for example, was designed to be a train in microcosm by combining both classes of passenger seating, luggage space, and guard's accommodation in a single coach. American combines had a similar purpose.

It obviously adds flavour to operations if *your* station is the one where trains are divided (and reconstituted when going in the opposite direction), but more vehicles are involved than just those mentioned above. A study of the prototype will reward you with new ideas. Horse boxes, milk tankers, and parcels, newspaper and postal vans are just a few examples of vehicles which might regularly be diagrammed for attachment to particular passenger trains.

Because of their emphasis on passenger traffic, British modellers tend to ignore the potential of their goods vehicles—tankers stand around without the assistance of hoses for discharging, low-loaders never get near an end-loading dock, and even cattle are sometimes expected to jump up from the ballast. In North America, the opposite is true, and layouts have developed mainly around the concept of freight operation and industries to be served. For example, introduce a furniture

factory and it will need regular supplies of wood, fabric, glues, glass, metal fittings, and possibly fuel to power its equipment. Apart from the empty vehicles that go off in search of their next load, the factory also despatches consignments of completed furniture. Breweries, chemical works, and other industries can similarly generate a wide range of movements, all with the clear purpose of serving the customer and making a profit for the railway. The more industries you find room for, the greater can be the variety and volume of traffic.

Avoid one trap, however. Modellers love to add new vehicles to their layouts, but they should not all be different. Even in earlier years, some vehicles tended to be found in small clusters, but particularly since the First World War there has been a tremendous increase in block trains composed entirely of the same or very similar vehicles: oil tankers, bulk cement, motor car components, high capacity mineral hoppers, and so on.

Another obvious aid to realism is to decide precisely which period you are modelling and keep to suitable stock. An American pike shouldn't be running Hi-cubes and Autoracks in the 1920s, while the few remaining 40ft boxcars were offi-

Rolling stock on an EM gauge layout by Andy Gibbs, representing the immediate pre-grouping period of British railways. This is clearly a portable track, as behind the Rothervale ore wagon can be seen a break which, unusually, passes across some pointwork. The difference between hand and rub-down lettering is evident.

cially devoid of roofwalks and had shortened end ladders by 1980. In Britain, clerestory stock is long gone and cattle traffic virtually extinct. Both were common in the 1920s. The use of vans and bogie stock has multiplied enormously, while private-owner wagons were eradicated by railway nationalisation, only to make a comeback recently. Even greater changes took place in Europe following war damage.

If you want to define a period, but have trouble deciding which it is to be, look again at the size of your layout. If space is at a premium, remember that older stock was shorter. Whereas four modern 75ft coaches may look self-conscious filling a station, six old-style 48ft coaches will fit the same space and be impressive. It is also easier to make room for shorter boxcars, etc., in the small yards that we must often accept. If you are still uncertain then build up separate sets of stock for different periods!

It is a good idea to begin operating by devising your own sequence timetable. It can be as simple as you care to make it, it works even for the smallest layout. It does not need a clock, simply remember how many vehicles fill each track! If operation really appeals to you, the schedules can be linked to a speeded-up clock; many demanding, but enjoyable, hours can be spent (especially with friends) struggling to keep the trains on time. Freight car forwarding systems are just as much fun. These are described fairly regularly in *Model Railroader* and *Railroad Model Craftsman*.

Modifying proprietary stock

So far we have been looking at what can be done with ready-to-run vehicles, but operation and the desire for realism quickly identify weaknesses, and several ways exist to counter these: rebuilding, kit-building, and scratch-building. Quite commonly, the techniques will be used together to produce the required model, so do not think of them in isolated cocoons, even though they are separately described below.

You often find that the family of coaches you need is available, but not the individual member. But if you study the vehicles that are produced, you may discover that one coach is similar enough to be cut up with a razor saw in a mitre box, and its sides reassembled with the sections in a different order to form the desired proto-

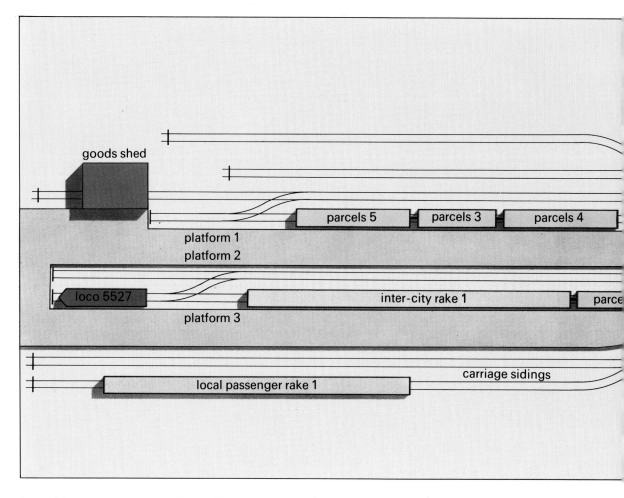

goods shed

parcels 5   parcels 3   parcels 4

platform 1
platform 2

loco 5527   inter-city rake 1   parce

platform 3

carriage sidings

local passenger rake 1

Some of the nomenclature and proportions of various trains and track-work. The length available for a station on a layout will often dictate the type and even period of railway which can reasonably be modelled. Freedom from some such restrictions contributes to the popularity of narrow-gauge layouts.

type. Generally it takes more than one coach to produce the new one, but with further thought you might be able to use the left-over pieces to convert another vehicle. Sheet polystyrene (plastic card) is an invaluable material for the modeller, and can be used to blank out (or reshape) an unwanted window. Body filler is then forced into the cracks and the whole insert rubbed down with very fine emery until it blends in with the surrounding panels. Continental and American streamlined coaches are less easy to cut up because it's difficult to hide blemishes in the corrugations, but window areas alone can be sawn out and moved, or you can even take out the entire section between any doors, slitting the body just inside the upper and lower corrugations, and replacing it with the new configuration.

Freight stock can similarly be altered. Tankers can be lengthened or shortened, extra bays added to hopper cars, vehicles forward- or back-dated by amending the giveaway features, and roofs (as a common American example) taken from one boxcar

to improve the accuracy of another.

While you are dealing with the big differences, of course, you might just as well sort out some of the little ones. Commercial vehicles (especially plastic ones) are inclined to suffer from manufacturing shortcuts. The most obvious of these is the handrail moulded on the body side. Where the rail is neatly executed, it may be wise to leave well alone, but if it is large and heavy, remove it with a *new* craft knife blade, file and fine emery paper, and replace it with brass or nickel silver wire. Chassis get very cavalier treatment, with totally wrong ones appearing under some bodies to get more use out of the moulds. Even if they are basically correct, the detail may be crude or skimpy, and you get a lot of satisfaction from fitting better scratch-built or cast details.

Inevitably, alterations will cause damage to any existing paintwork. If the damage is beyond a discreet touch-up, you can strip paint off plastic vehicles by immersing them for a few hours in car brake fluid (e.g. Castrol Girling). An old

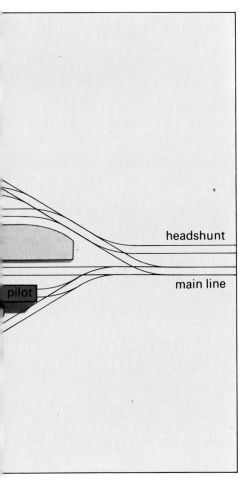

headshunt

main line

pilot

although they do have 'body', which can be useful at times. Liquid solvents are much more easily controlled and applied with a fine brush (though not all plastics respond to them) and make very neat joints if brushed on from the hidden side. Use the solvent sparingly and do not press hard; the solvent melts the plastic and any excess takes longer to dry and bubbles may form. The solvent can also attack the detail and may produce a weaker bond. Plastic glue can badly damage the side of a vehicle if you get it on your fingers. You may salvage this with body filler, but the kit could be a write-off. Using unsuitable glues is another way to ruin a model.

Wooden kits are still quite common in America, and offer few difficulties in assembly, in fact their design may make it easy to add extra detailing, especially to the chassis. One thing that does require care, however, is the preparation for painting. If you are trying to turn out a supposedly metal vehicle, a smooth finish is essential, so give it two or three coats of sanding sealer, rubbing down with very fine carborundum paper or with a glass fibre brush. The fine particles of glass which result from the latter should be allowed to fall on to an old newspaper and be wrapped up and carefully disposed of. Your hands should be rinsed under run-

One of the first considerations in determining how much rolling stock etc. is needed is to work out a timetable or sequence of movements. A simple binder of movement cards hung on the track will act as a challenge to visiting friends, and later actual times to be met can be included.

toothbrush will remove those patches that have not completely dissolved.

Kit-building

The simplest kits on the market are plastic, some coming already painted and lettered. American freight car kits are available which even the newest modeller can assemble with a knife, glue, and a screwdriver in under 15 minutes. More commonly, kits have 20–50 parts on a series of plastic sprues. These *can* be put together in less than half an hour, but the result will not be very impressive; time taken in preparation always leads to a better finish. Do not twist parts off their sprues; saw them off and clean away the stubs with a file. Any flash (the surplus material squeezed out where moulds separate) should be carefully trimmed away. Certain parts are more easily (and thoroughly) painted before the model goes together, but do not paint surfaces which will have to be glued.

When assembly does commence, you will discover that cements are messy,

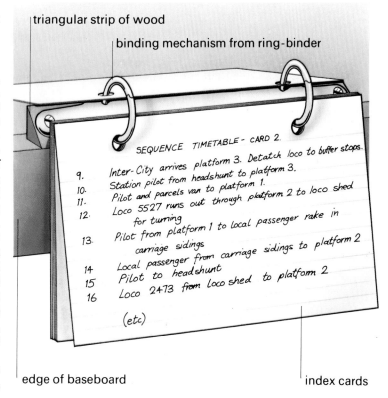

triangular strip of wood

binding mechanism from ring-binder

SEQUENCE TIMETABLE - CARD 2.

9. Inter-City arrives platform 3. Detatch loco to buffer stops.
10. Station pilot from headshunt to platform 3.
11. Pilot and parcels van to platform 1.
12. Loco 5527 runs out through platform 2 to loco shed for turning
13. Pilot from platform 1 to local passenger rake in carriage sidings
14. Local passenger from carriage sidings to platform 2
15. Pilot to headshunt
16. Loco 2473 from loco shed to platform 2

(etc)

edge of baseboard

index cards

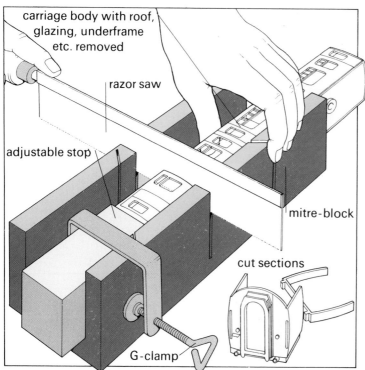

carriage body with roof, glazing, underframe etc. removed

razor saw

adjustable stop

mitre-block

cut sections

G-clamp

Cutting coach bodies accurately for readjustment of window/door order or addition of new sections requires an accurate mitre block and a positive means of holding the body. Some plastics tend to jam the saw teeth and this can cause the body to move unless it is firmly clamped in place.

ning water without rubbing them together. Ignoring these suggestions may lead to several hours of skin irritation. Thin card can be used to cover a rather roughly-cut roof if necessary, while a layer of tissue paper gives a nice representation of a canvas-covered roof.

Kits that mix materials (particularly things like acetates) offer another problem of bonding, and contact adhesives seem to be the most successful. But you must be certain that both partners in the bond will accept the adhesive. It will often be found that three or four different glues are needed when tackling kits of this type.

Some really attractive vehicles can be made from aluminium kits. The metal punches fairly readily, and if done carefully, very little distortion arises from the stresses involved. It is also easy to shape aluminium, but this is a two-edged advantage since it will also dent and scar, so treat it gently. Although it will accept the right solder, it does not particularly like it, and it is quite capable of shearing away from adhesives which you felt sure would hold it. The problem is that aluminium has its own built-in chemical shield which makes it a very slippery metal. It re-establishes itself very swiftly if allowed to. Preparation is therefore important: rub the metal down with fine emery *immediately* before bonding with Araldite or a similar epoxy,

pausing only to wipe away any aluminium dust. When drilling the metal, use a drop of washing-up liquid to lubricate the cutting edges, or the swarf will wrap round the drill. When painting aluminium, rub it down as before with fine emery paper, and use a self-etching primer. Take a little care with the painting, and the final appearance should be well worth your trouble.

Though little used elsewhere, white metal revolutionised the British kit market. While the concentration is on locomotives, many wagons and several coaches have also appeared. It requires a low investment, so even obscure prototypes can be profitable, but the quality of the products is highly variable, arising from (i) the original masters, (ii) shrinkage while cooling, (iii) mould compression, (iv) mould degradation, and (v) the grade of metal used. The appearance of your final model therefore depends on good preparation.

Flash can be trimmed away with a knife and filed clean. Minor mis-matching in the mould produces ridges which should be filed away unless they are too severe. Cylindrical objects in particular may be distorted: if they become too slender after cleaning up, a thin wrapping of cigarette paper may save them, but this obviously depends on the component. If the model is poorly detailed, some enhancement may be possible. The vehicle will always look better when painted, but your time might be better spent in constructing replacement parts. Mould degradation is also a factor in this; the rubber moulds wear out quickly, and flash appears on the face of the castings. Careful work with a chisel-bladed knife and an ordinary pointed blade can work wonders. And if you get small pitting in a flat surface, rubbing gently with a smooth spoon handle might cure it; if not, use a car body filler.

When assembling, check that straight sides are truly straight; if not, *gentle* finger pressure will correct them. Epoxy will make an excellent bond (after checking that parts fit properly), and you can solder if you use a cool iron and low-melt solder or otherwise know what you are doing. A better choice, however, is car body filler, which can make the joint invisible. About ten minutes after applying, use a sharp knife to cut away the surplus filler, peeling it away even from rivet detail that was accidentally covered. Be careful because the joint is still fragile and must not be stressed. Occasional prodding of left-over filler will indicate when the knife will cut cleanly.

An important newcomer is the etched-brass kit. Being derived from photographic reductions of large scale drawings means that even modestly-skilled craftsmen can incorporate very fine details in them. The etching process introduces certain limitations; it cannot easily reproduce deep framing or a thick buffer-beam, for example. Most of these limitations can be overcome, however, so that a reasonably competent person can turn out models of almost museum standard from the better kits in about a fortnight.

The parts are held on a series of frets and should only be detached as required; the smaller ones can otherwise be difficult to identify and disappear readily. Separation can be done with tinsnips, a piercing saw or a small chisel and mallet, and the remainder of the tab should be filed away or it may prevent a good fit during assembly. Glue can be used, but a far

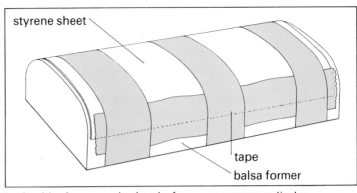

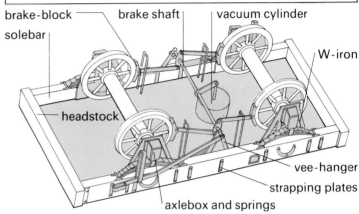

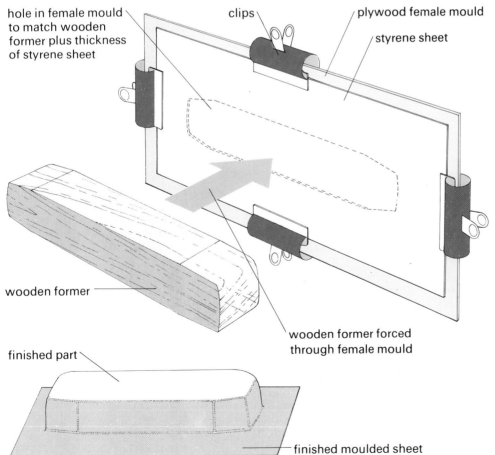

hole in female mould to match wooden former plus thickness of styrene sheet

clips

plywood female mould

styrene sheet

wooden former

wooden former forced through female mould

finished part

finished moulded sheet

Above: Permanent curves can be induced by strapping styrene sheet to a wooden former and boiling it for two or three minutes. The lower drawing shows the chassis of a four-wheel van of the sort recommended for an initial attempt at scratch building. Details of how to tackle it appear overleaf.

Left: Moulding coach roofs and ends, or similar items, is not difficult using this method. Styrene softens suddenly at just above water boiling point; using an electric fire or radiant plate is best. Take care! More than one heating may be needed. Draw deeper than necessary so that cockling can be cut off.

stronger model results from soldering the main bodywork. In the later stages it is a matter of choice: grabrails can be soldered, but some fine details may prove difficult to attach if the iron is being forced to heat up a large surrounding area. After limited success with rapid epoxy (it dried so fast that 90% was wasted), it was found that with 24-hour epoxy small quantities could be applied where needed with the tip of a pin, and then the fine details manoeuvred into place with tweezers. It is better to have no surplus glue, but careful use of a knife (being careful not to scar the brass) will chip it away. Rub the finished body with a glass-fibre brush and coat with self-etch primer to give the paint a key.

Scratch-building goods vehicles

Scratch-building has now been made simpler by the vast improvements in the materials themselves (the introduction of polystyrene sheet and quick, effective glues) and the availability of components which avoid difficult jobs or save you tasks which you do not enjoy. Only when entering competitions does it matter how much of a hybrid your model is!

The beginner might start with a 4-wheel van, marking out on a styrene sheet about 0.040in (1mm) thick. Where possible, planking lines are scored at this point; the ridges which result are rubbed down with a smooth file or emery, and the grooves cleaned out again. When marking out, incidentally, make allowance for the styrene's thickness. You can mitre the vehicle's corners, but it is easier to narrow the ends and fit them between the sides, or vice versa. If possible, try to hide the joint under later detail such as corner strapping.

Assemble sides and ends around a wood or styrene floor, and fit a false ceiling to prevent the sides bowing in as the solvent dries out. Next make the doors and framing, building up in layers, and then construct ribs to support the roof. You can curve 10–20 thou (0.25–0.5mm) styrene by hand, but a better way is to tape it down securely to a piece of shaped balsa wood and drop it into *boiling* water. Detach it from the balsa wood after 2–3 minutes, trim to size, and glue it to the van body when dry. Make riveted plates with a blunt scriber, pressing it into the back of 5 thou styrene before detaching from the main sheet. The remaining details can then be manufactured from styrene, rod, and wire.

If cast axleguards are used, their design will determine the width between the chassis solebars when related to the wheels, axles, and bearings. Both solebars should be fitted at this stage, then two axleguards to the *same* solebar at the correct spacing. When these are firm, the wheelsets can be added and opposite axleguards glued in place, individually or together. Ensure that the axles are parallel to one another, and before the glue sets solid, check that all four wheels touch a perfectly flat surface.

The strongest part of the remaining chassis should be the V-hangers, which support the brake gear and the rod across to the opposite side. The easiest approach is to cut each V from one piece of styrene. You could, however, shape both Vs from a length of metal, fixed to the bottom of the floor and folded down at each side. This helps with the brake lever, which may be easier to shape from metal than styrene. The brake shoes require careful filing, but otherwise the remaining chassis work is simple after doctoring the buffer shanks to clear the solebars.

Bogie freight vehicles are not much more complex than four-wheel vehicles in many cases—just longer and more repetitive! American modellers will need ladders and roofwalks for older boxcars (and will probably buy in the mesh types where available). The removal of roofwalks and shortening of ladders in recent years would have been useful if roof designs had not grown more complex in the meantime. But if you cannot saw the right roof off a commercial model, stanway diagonal and x-panels can be built up from styrene—possibly shaped in a jig to relieve tedious repetition. Drill styrene ladder uprights as a pair and insert rods for the rungs, or solder wire and pins in a simple jig for the slender types.

Plug doors and sliding doors are rather daunting at first sight, but closer examination reveals that most can be built up from lengths and rectangles of styrene sheet or rod. Corrugated car ends may be more problematical, but if unobtainable separately, could be 'borrowed' from a cheap commercial product. If you are compelled to build the ends from scratch, consider the possibility of turning out one really good master so that you can cast enough for several vehicles.

Modern vehicles, British, European and American, may have a central spine or girder construction which can be reproduced in wood, styrene or card with little difficulty. Indeed some American types in particular are so shrouded by their bodies that you might only fit the skimpiest detail. Older stock is less amenable, with clearly visible queen posts and truss rods. These can be produced in styrene, but metal is a better answer, and a detachable metal sub-assembly holding all the queen posts and trusses would be stronger, yet be easily repairable if it did get damaged.

Even for scratch-built models, Americans normally buy complete trucks (bogies) while British modellers buy white metal castings. If the type you want is not available, and you can build a nickel silver or brass master, some firms will do castings for you (especially if allowed to add them to their own range). You can do home casting with resins, or fret out all your needs from metal. The latter takes time but will be as good as you can make it. Solder or clamp the sideframe blanks together, to saw and drill them as a single unit. When the basic outline is right, separate the side-frames and detail them—laminations for leaf springs, screw

threads for coils, washers and discs for bearings, wire for tie-rods, and so on. For ease of working, keep the axleboxes on the stock length of material while filing to shape. Make stretchers and bolsters, insert the wheels, and then 'tune' the bogies until they run freely.

This section has largely assumed the use of styrene, but especially as you progress to tankers, hoppers and other more exotic vehicles, keep an open mind about the material which will give the best result.

Passenger stock

Coachbuilders in 0 gauge and above prefer wood or metal for robustness, but in the smaller scales they are uncommon except where they offer a particular advantage (e.g. veneer to represent teak), and the use of card is also disappearing. Acrylic sheet (like Perspex or Plexiglas) has been used for coach sides, but curved profiles require a lot of sanding, and the windows have to be protected from abrasion, from clouding when attaching the outer face of the body-work, and during painting.

With its ease of working, it is not sur-

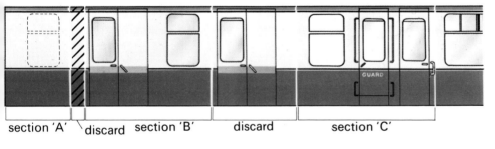

section 'A' \discard section 'B' discard section 'C'

cut new window

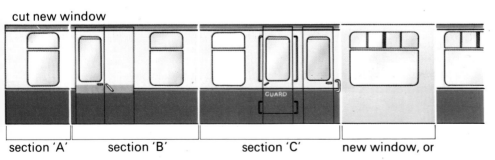

section 'A' section 'B' section 'C' new window, or

Slicing up coaches and rearranging the pieces or inserting new sections is simpler than scratch-building complete vehicles, and provided fine and accurate sawcuts are made is not as difficult as it may sound. Corrugated construction is trickier, since it is not easy to hide blemishes in the corrugations, but windows can be changed (bottom drawing).

section from another vehicle

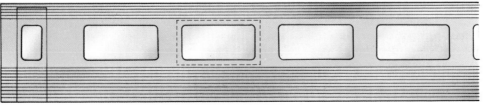

prising that styrene is once again the favourite material. Slab-sided coaches differ little from boxcars except for the windows and the fact that the interior is visible. Most joints are square and at right-angles, permitting swift and sound construction. Curved sides are less amenable, and if bent while cold will eventually straighten. Either boil them on a former, as described earlier, or laminate several thin pieces while the shape is held.

A curved side may also be used for panelled stock. The beading is drawn out on 5–10 thou (0.125–0.25mm) styrene. As most beading has rounded corners, these are drilled out and linked with a very sharp blade. If the beading on the opposite side of the coach is identical or a mirror of the first side, both can be drilled (but not cut) together. When all the panels are removed, the lacework of beading is incredibly fragile. Any stress (e.g. the drag of a blunt knife) will stretch the styrene so it won't lie flat. If this does happen, you may be able to remove a wafer of material to settle it down. Minor knife damage may also be remedied; if the sides of the cut can be smoothed over, the solvent's welding action may obliterate it. One other point: the lacework is so fine that very little solvent is required, and *none* should reach your fingers while you position it!

One approach to corrugated sides is to find an old saw blade with the right pitch of teeth. Stone the teeth to the shape you need, and snap off a piece of blade to the length required. Secure it in a hand vice, press it against a straight edge clamped along the coach side, and draw it gently over the styrene so that each tooth digs a furrow. You may require several passes, so be careful not to wobble; you should also expect some failures (including digging too deep), but persevere. Boil the styrene if a curve is needed—cold forming will fracture the sides.

Thin single-skin coach sides welded to internal bulkheads will probably pull, leaving a vertical line down the outside of the body after the joint hardens. Sandwich construction cures this problem and retains the glazing at the same time. Each side has two skins, the inner one sometimes with larger apertures. A glazing strip

A London North Western full parcels brake. Features include a guard's position in the centre (hence the corridor connection at the end) and panels painted matt grey on which could be chalked details of contents and destinations. In service the white roof tended to discolour rather quickly.

runs the length of the sides, between the skins, with a packing strip of the same thickness above and below the window area. Alternatively, the lower body may be packed as before, but the upper section has vertical packing between the windows, while the windows themselves are individual drop-in panes. If the roof is removable, damaged 'glass' can be changed. Some people use glass in their models, but clear plastic is more usual. Do not use acetate which buckles when it expands.

The easiest coach ends are non-corridor types, and may be no more than a single styrene bulkhead, styrene steps and a few scraps of wire for grab rails. If a coach is being built from metal, however, a good way is to shape the steps on a stock length of brass angle, separating each with the final strokes of the file. On corridor stock, the gangway (diaphragm) bellows can be folded from good quality paper, cut to go round the three visible sides. Rigid bellows can be detailed easily, but working ones will need more thought. Styrene provides the gangway doors, and tissues the tarpaulin over the top.

Open platform ends are not too difficult, but it may prove easier to jig-build the railings, or pin them into balsa while soldering. With observation coaches, the problem is building a strong enough framework for the glazing—unless the design is so slab sided that the structure itself can be clear plastic, and the framing purely decorative. Those with lots of curved panes may require heating over a former, possibly in two or three stages.

Contoured roofs may be obtainable as component spin-offs from kits, but scratch-built roofs need not be difficult. Simple contours can be hand-rolled, heat formed, or sanded from wood, and overlaid with paper or thin card. Solid-sided monitor roofs can be two slabs of wood, profiled as required, but the clerestory equivalent needs different treatment if it is to pass light. The centre section could be a block of acrylic, with low half-roofs on each side, but the usual treatment is to extend the clerestory sides downwards to make a good bond with the half roofs, then glue the upper section across the top.

Before fitting the roof, do you want an

interior? Those building showcase models obviously will, and may fit simulated or real veneer woodwork, carpets cut from advertisement pages or colour photographs, seats cast in white metal or epoxy resin, and upholstery, blinds, luggage racks, and so on. At the other extreme, working coaches which will not be lit could do without interiors altogether, so long as visible partitions are in place. The usual compromise is to fit seats of approximately the right shape and colour, and perhaps add 'mirrors' from chrome tape, and 'photographs' from paper rectangles with sepia ink vaguely suggesting landscapes.

Older coach chassis are a joy to look at (or a nightmare, according to your point of view!) but would demand considerable time if they were modelled in their entirety, so it is probable that more omissions are made here than on any other part of the exterior. If you are inclined to simplify, model those areas which are prominently visible, plus those which might irritate you if they were missing (e.g. generators and brake cylinders). As with freight stock girdering is straightforward, but queen posts and truss rods are difficult to make robustly without being overscale. Cylinders can be lathe-turned if you have the facilities, or be manufactured from wood dowelling and cigarette paper. The paper should be attached by its plain end to the wood with only a trace of glue, and then wrapped round. The adhesive at the other end is dampened to secure it, and the result is a smooth cylinder which can be added to the model and painted without further preparation. Install a few lengths of wire running in the right direction (but surreptitiously anchored where they disappear from view) and you should persuade most onlookers that all the brake gear has been fitted.

Batteries can be fabricated in wood or styrene, but if you make up a complete styrene box, drill a small hole in the back. This lets the solvent fumes escape, lessening the chance that welding stresses will

draw the box concave. The bogies can be made as outlined earlier, but try to use a fairly wide bearing between the bogie and the coach body to dampen movement. You want the vehicle to run loosely enough to cope with undulating track, but not so sloppy that it tilts to one side then bounces to the other as it rolls along.

Painting

Most painting is still done by brush, but spraying with an airbrush is getting more common. People generally find that, although spraying brings its own problems of spatter and orange-peel finishes if the paint consistency is wrong, they still tend to get a much better finish than with a brush (especially since the introduction of quick-drying paints). A wide range of prototype-matched colours is available, though most are enamels which cover well but are less easy to use for lining out. One answer is to line with water-based paint, another to use cellulose from touch-up cans supplied for minor car repairs. This

lines neatly, but dislikes enamel and attacks styrene. However, building up the first colour in several coats permits the etching agents to evaporate safely away, leaving a barrier layer for further coats.

Professional model-makers mainly use a draughtsman's bow pen for lining, but straight lines can be painted between strips of clear adhesive tape, or lining tape can be used if you can get the right colour. Lettering transfers (decals) are available for better known railway companies in Britain and America (and in a few cases for Continental prototypes), but modellers of the lesser-known ones must either use similar lettering intended for other companies, or paint everything themselves. A major exception to this in America is the existence of custom decal manufacturers who will turn out designs based on customers' artwork—very valuable when one remembers the high percentage of fictitious railroads in model form. Standard dimensional data decals can also be obtained. The nearest British counterpart is the

Old-time combination baggage and passenger car of a pattern widely used all over the United States. The clerestory roof gave overhead light and additional headroom for passengers making their way along the centre aisle of the car. Yellow was a popular colour and is still used on several of the major American railroads.

Interior detail in an 0 gauge combination car being built for Robert Hegge's Crooked Mountain Lines. Producing the number of wooden armrests required is a challenge in itself. Although Pullman coaches have been seen complete down to the cutlery, for most modellers a suggestion of basic features is adequate.

Private Owner wagon, of which there used to be several hundred thousand; while a tiny sample are obtainable as kits or ready-to-run, in the main the liveries must be produced by hand, assisted by one limited range of correctly shaded alphabets and whatever can be used from Letraset and similar rub-on lettering. However, the presence of such wagons adds great appeal and individuality to a layout, and they provide the rare opportunity to freelance in a British context.

Beautiful though they may look when painting is complete, the fact is that models in a pristine finish are unrealistic, and more and more modellers are accepting the need to weather their vehicles. But do not apply an overall, even layer of dirt before you look at the real thing. Most dirt is thrown up vertically from the track and thins out towards roof level. Other streaking tends to follow joints and edges in the metal, the first places where rust gets a hold. Variations arise from the areas

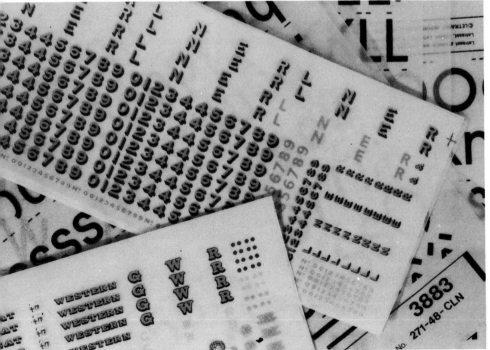

The availability of rub-down lettering in a variety of styles, including sheets produced specifically for railway modellers, has eased enormously the problem of a neat finish on locomotives and rolling stock. The sheets shown are from Letraset.

Overleaf: A scene from a 00 layout which includes quite a selection of rolling stock. Sixty years or so ago 'mixed freight' trains included all sorts of vans, wagons, tankers and the like, and even trains of coal wagons had variety in the private owners' liveries. Modern freight trains tend to be more restricted to 'one of a kind' vehicles.

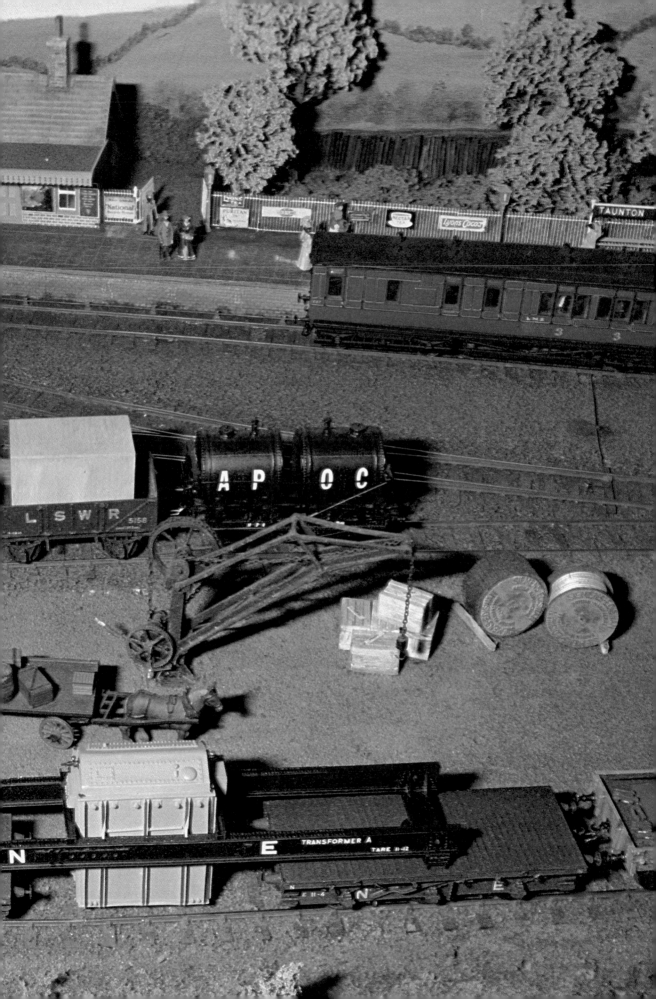

Compensation is a matter of allowing axles to tilt; instead of the fixed axles (1) giving a bumpy ride, both axles tilting (2) or one tilting axle (and acceptance of a tilting floor) as in (3) will provide smoother and quieter operation as well as, frequently, longer life for the vehicles. Model details are shown at (5).

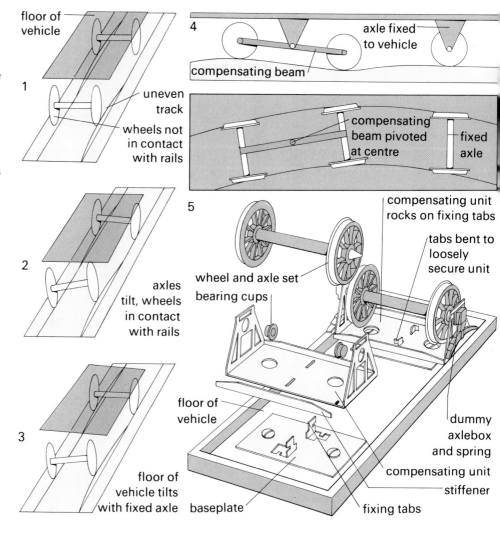

floor of vehicle

1

uneven track

wheels not in contact with rails

2

axles tilt, wheels in contact with rails

3

floor of vehicle tilts with fixed axle

4

axle fixed to vehicle

compensating beam

compensating beam pivoted at centre

fixed axle

5

compensating unit rocks on fixing tabs

tabs bent to loosely secure unit

wheel and axle set

bearing cups

floor of vehicle

baseplate

dummy axlebox and spring

compensating unit stiffener

fixing tabs

usually traversed—i.e. the predominant rock colour—and messy loads carried, such as white clays and dusty gravels. Do not over-weather, and keep paints fairly thin—the original colour ought to be visible through most of the muck. Once you're satisfied, protect the finish with matt varnish.

Couplings and performance

The unsuitability or inefficiency of couplings can go a long way towards killing the enjoyment of a layout, especially if it is supposed to feature the kind of operation outlined earlier. Options include hornhook, Kadee, Continental, Hornby, Peco, three-link, and Alex Jackson. Of these only three-link is truly accurate to prototype, but all types make a compromise between accuracy, efficiency, and the realities of working in small scales without miniature

personnel to assist. In the USA, Kadees are the principal alternative to commercial hornhooks, and as they are more sophisticated, the change is frequently made. In Britain the names are confusing but the situation is clear: the old Hornby–Dublo coupling was largely suppressed by Hornby (ex-Tri-ang) whose own coupling was rather more reliable but much more ugly. Peco continue to make a Hornby–Dublo-type coupling for those who prefer it. The three-link coupling (and the screw coupling for passenger stock) requires the operator's constant attention with bits of bent wire. It can be beautiful to watch a freight train take up the slack as it pulls away from a dead stand; but after intensively working a terminus station during a three-day exhibition, I would be reluctant to fit such couplings to my own small scale stock. The virtually invisible

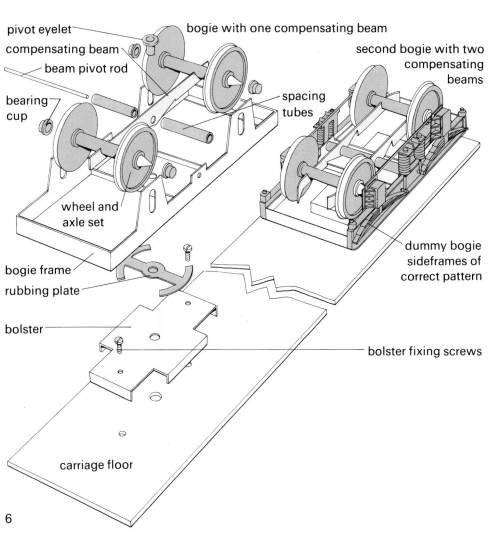

pivot eyelet

compensating beam

beam pivot rod

bearing cup

bogie with one compensating beam

second bogie with two compensating beams

spacing tubes

wheel and axle set

bogie frame

rubbing plate

bolster

dummy bogie sideframes of correct pattern

bolster fixing screws

carriage floor

6

The same principle of compensation applied to passenger stock provides a much more comfortable ride, which in model terms means more reliable running and fewer derailments. Fitting compensating beams inside dummy sideframes allows all four wheels of a bogie to remain in contact with the track.

Alex Jackson coupling has been operated in the same conditions with great enjoyment. However, it is home-made and very fragile, although a more robust commercial version has recently been marketed.

Most commercial couplings space vehicles too far apart, and it is less than realistic to have airy gaps between coaches that are supposedly corridor-connected. If the coaches can be kept as set rakes, the normal couplings can be removed and solid bars substituted. These are attached loosely to screws or press studs underneath each vehicle end. Because the coaches then move very little, relative to one another, more convincing gangways can be fitted and be rarely disturbed, but the press stud arrangement permits the coaches to be split for storage. Each end of the rake does of course have standard couplings to con-

nect with the rest of the stock.

However good-looking your models and efficient their couplings, in the final analysis they must run well. Obvious points are to keep wheels clean; lubricate even pin-point axles (but sparingly) and check doubtful runners for squareness in the chassis, fluff or paint in the bearings, damage to flanges, and other components rubbing against the wheels (see the chapter on Maintenance). It also makes vehicle behaviour more reliable if you weight them evenly. My own target in 4mm scale is one ounce per axle, while the NMRA recommends one ounce plus half an ounce per inch of vehicle length. Either way, vehicles are more willing to stay on the track when shunted, hauled round tight curves, or propelled over complex pointwork; that makes the whole railway more enjoyable to operate.

Overleaf: Less common vehicles include specialised transporters and railway equipment such as breakdown cranes. This one, in H0 gauge, is by Jouef and the crane mechanism works. The flat boom support truck is part of a complete breakdown train offered by this French company and appeals strongly to younger enthusiasts.

Right: Container wagon for beer (and other liquids) produced by Fleischmann in H0 scale.

Below: German Railways 10-ton crane-wagon, from Fleischmann.

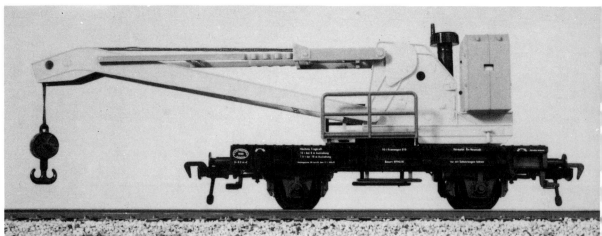

Right: Another Fleischmann model, an automatic discharge hopper wagon with removable roof.

Top: Märklin's German Railways' small Transporter for cars, in H0 scale.

Above: An open wagon with brakeman's cab from the same manufacturer.

Left: Flat wagon (or flat car) with lorry load, German Railways, by Fleischmann.

Left: A 40-foot double decker stock car in H0 by American maker Athearn.

Right: A 42-foot work flat car of the Southern Pacific by Walters (USA).

Below: Liliput make this H0 Compagnie Internationale des Wagons Lit dining car.

Right: Unusual French double-decker coaches by Jouef.

Above: Spanish passenger coach of 1930, of the former Madrid-Zaragoza-Alicante line, by Electrotren.

Left: Tankers are common traffic. This is for phosphorus for the Victor Chemical Co. Made by Athearn.

Right: A wood-finish main line LNER carriage by the British manufacturer Graham Farish.

Right: Lima produces stock of many nationalities; this is a 00 coach in British Railways livery.

Right: A covered carriage truck of about 1937 by Lima, in the early British Railways colours.

Right: The same vehicle as above, but this time finished in the contemporary LMS livery.

Left: A Pullman dining/parlour coach in the famous Brighton Belle colours, by Wrenn.

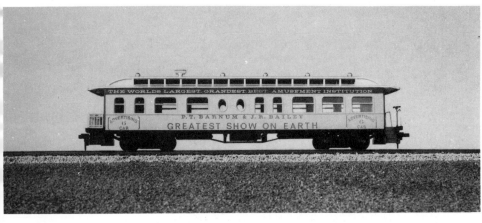

Left: H0 Daylight coach of the Southern Pacific Railroad by the U.S. manufacturer Athearn.

Left: Also from Athearn is this period circus coach, part of a Barnum and Bailey train.

Left: Tyco, another well-known American maker, offer this early Western and Atlantic passenger car.

KEEPING IT RUNNING

Whether models are 'ready-to-run' or 'proto scale', there is a need for maintenance and its standard must be kept as high as possible if the hobby is going to be enjoyable. Care and attention of all equipment, from the surface on which the track is laid through to the locomotives and rolling stock, will determine the degree of enjoyment. The trains all need to be cared for whether they are run only occasionally and then put back in their box, or permanently left on the track. The points to be made in this chapter relate to all types of locomotives and rolling stock.

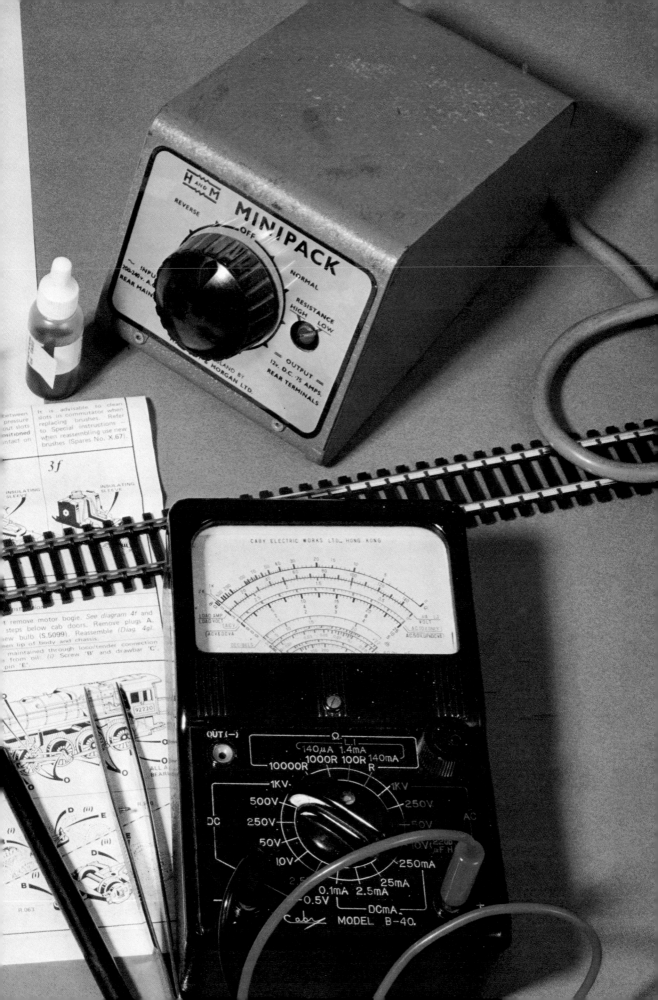

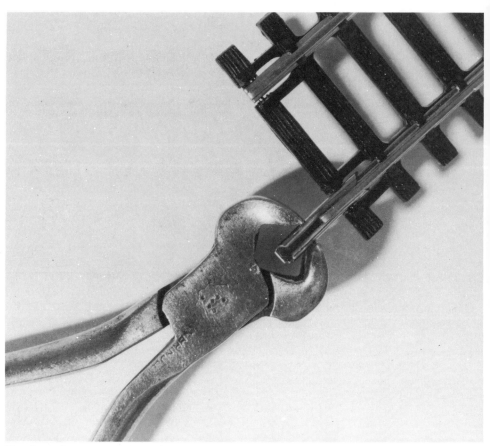

Track maintenance

The provision of a suitable surface, whether temporary or permanent is not within the scope of this chapter. Temporary tracks are usually laid on the floor (despite warnings against the practice by every manufacturer) or on the largest available table; the very fact of frequent assembly and dismantling contributes to possible trouble. Permanent, or semi-permanent tracks are much less likely to cause difficulties, especially if basic rules have been followed throughout the construction stage.

Except in the unlikely event of a track specially made in one piece, there must be joints; the more joints which there are in an electrical circuit, the more chance there is of trouble. Every stage, from the mains plug on the wall to the locomotive moving along the track should be checked regularly and carefully. With the usual 12-volt system, a frequent source of trouble is the connections from the controller to the track; they should be tight and clean. If possible, the output wires should be soldered to the track, even if sectional track is being used on an 'as-required' basis, to reduce the number of 'plug-together' connections. Good soldering requires absolute cleanliness, adequate flux and a hot iron which leaves a bright patch of solder rather than an amorphous grey blob which could develop into a 'dry' joint and a source of future failure. If a power-connecting clip must be used, an occasional rub with a track cleaner or fine abrasive paper over the contact areas beneath the rails will help, followed by a very light smear of Vaseline or other petroleum jelly.

Having introduced the power at a particular point it must pass along and remain constant to all parts of the layout. Joiners, or fishplates, are commonly used at joins in the rails, serving the dual purposes of aligning the joints to prevent derailments and passing the electrical current. On permanent layouts where joins will be connected only once there should be no problems. Because the layout is permanent, bonds can be made across each join to ensure current continuity, except, of course, at section gaps which are intended to break continuity.

Where sectional track is used, especially when a layout is temporary and has to be put away after each session, all electrical contact will be through the joiners (fish-plates). Reduce the number of joins which have to be broken and made by keeping as many sections as possible connected together. If this is inconvenient, all track pieces will inevitably suffer wear and tear, and to maintain them in good condition care should be taken in joining and breaking. Each dismantling will add to the chance of a voltage drop. If a reduction of current occurs every joint is suspect. Joiners which become loose-fitting or damaged should be checked to see if gentle squeezing with a pair of pliers will solve the problem, but if there is any doubt they should be replaced. Manufacturers sell packets of spares, but if those for a particular make are not easily available, the local dealer will no doubt be able to offer others which are virtually identical.

Compatibility of track components is relatively recent. Even 15 years ago some-one wanting to buy, say, a wagon for a gift had to know almost exactly what make and system the recipient used. Major differences in systems made things difficult to an extent hard to realise by a present-day newcomer who is offered common track, common wheel standard and common couplings (compatible rather than identical), all two-rail and becoming closer all the time.

Modern points (turnouts) are 'self-isolating', which means that they feed electricity in the direction in which they are set while the other part is dead, or isolated. This is usually achieved by the point blade picking up current from the stock rail which it touches. Sometimes when a locomotive is run over a point it will stop dead, and the easiest way to check whether the point itself is at fault is to try another locomotive or, if no locomotive is available, check with two wires connected to a bulb. Provided that the layout is not permanent, it is easy to remove the point and check the contact, cleaning it and adding a tiny smear of petroleum jelly. If the point is of the type using a small spring copper contact, use extreme care to adjust the contact.

Locomotives and rolling stock

Ever since the birth of Hornby Dublo it has become usual to include some form of guidance on keeping things running with every set or separate locomotive. Advice is normally included on what to do before

Rail-cleaning rubbers are similar to conventional erasers but contain a very fine abrasive calculated to clean the track without damage. Removal of the debris after rubbing along a rail is necessary, and a soft brush or a car vacuum cleaner would be suitable. Occasional light use is better than acquiring a heavy deposit.

the locomotive is used together with routine maintenance and often hints on fault finding.

Discussing the lubrication of every type of model is neither practical nor necessary, but, whatever set or locomotive may have been bought, please read the instructions; they are written to help you get the best from the trains. Generally, before running, it is just a case of light lubrication of running parts. In early days it was customary for a small bottle of oil to be supplied and the recommended way of applying it was with a needle or pin. By this means it was fairly easy to apply and the tiny drop which hung on the end of the pin was the ideal amount.

As the rest of the rolling stock is added, it is as well to check that the wheels are free-running. With modern production methods, wagon chassis and coach bogies are usually moulded in one piece, and because they are mass-produced and packed quickly, sometimes an axle is held a little tight. Generally gentle outward pressure with the fingers is enough to cure the problem, but be careful and make continual checks so that it isn't overdone. While doing this the wheels should be spun to make sure that they are true. Although

many makes use metal axles and metal (or at least metal-tyred) wheels which run very well, a minority use plastic wheels and axles moulded in one piece, which, when new, need little attention or lubrication. There is a faint possibility that some plastics may react adversely to applications of oil, but if this is the case the maker's instructions should refer to this.

The only other items needing a quick check are the couplings. All ready-to-run types now have variations on the hook and loop pattern and a casual check should be enough. With plastic components a small moulding flash may possibly interfere with free action, but careful trimming with a very sharp knife is simple.

In some of the older instruction manuals, certain maintenance items had a time scale, which was all very well if the owner kept a log of the running times of the models. Maintenance often did not get done until things went wrong. So many factors affect the performance of a locomotive that, while some routine maintenance is desirable, it is very difficult to say at what intervals it should be done. In this respect model railways do not differ from other fields in which servicing is carried out at irregular intervals.

A fairly typical chassis for a locomotive— compare with the drawing on page 132. The red portion is the armature windings and the commutator and brushes are just to the left. Gently cleaning out the slots in the commutator with a pointed matchstick often works wonders. Note the weight carried to improve adhesion.

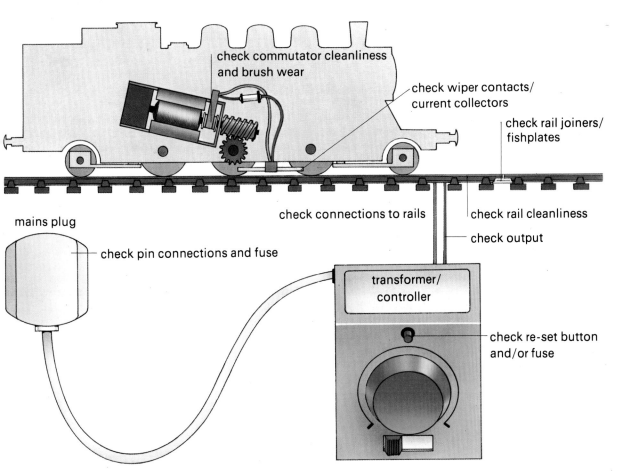

check commutator cleanliness and brush wear

check wiper contacts/ current collectors

check rail joiners/ fishplates

mains plug

check pin connections and fuse

check connections to rails

check rail cleanliness

check output

transformer/ controller

check re-set button and/or fuse

Locomotives often need running in, and one of the advantages of the simple oval layout is that this can be done under operating conditions. A recent introduction by a manufacturer of train controllers is a cradle which allows this to be done on a bed of rollers. Either method is preferable to turning the model upside-down and merely holding two wires for contact, since this does not allow the locomotive to perform under operating conditions and true running cannot be observed. Normally half an hour of steady running will work wonders on what may start out as a rather stiff and erratic performer.

Most of the previous comments have been angled towards the ready-to-run locomotive, but running-in is also the ideal way for a scratch-builder to try out a chassis. Small adjustments can be made which will later make all the difference to the operation of the locomotive.

Once run in, maintenance will depend on the way that the trains are used and how often; those used when first bought and then left neglected for months or even years are bound to perform differently from those in regular use. This also applies to those used on the floor, especially on carpet. Trains used on temporary layouts should be packed away with care, preferably in the original packing. Furthermore, when trains become old enough to interest collectors the original packing adds considerably to the value! Apart from this, it will keep dirt out and protect the couplings. Always keep the instructions with the models in the box.

Cleaning

Even with all this care there will be some wear and tear. The main snag with the track itself is likely to be dirt; when nice and new the surface will be clean, but after a very short time it will start to get dirty. Modern tracks are mainly nickel silver, but even the steel type have improved and dirt takes longer to accumulate. Look at, say, the old grey-based Tri-ang track from the early days of two-rail, in any shop selling second-hand trains—it needed cleaning virtually every time it was used.

If wiped regularly with a rag impregnated with methylated spirit (alcohol) the dirt build-up won't get thick or hard enough to give any trouble, but if neglected

Checking for continuity of current supply is straightforward; it helps if an inexpensive meter is available but two wires and a bulb will do—except of course for mains supply! If the track is receiving current the fault must lie in the locomotive mechanism or the collection of current from the track.

it will become too stubborn for this method. The answer then is a track-cleaning rubber, which is rather like an ordinary eraser but contains abrasive powder and should be available from your model shop. The abrasive is very fine and will do the job well; don't be tempted to use glasspaper or even carborundum paper, since these will start to take off any anti-corrosive coating the manufacturer may have applied and will eventually make the problem worse. Extra care must be taken when cleaning points, to avoid damaging the mechanism. After cleaning, by any method, check for any cleaning material left behind.

The other point of contact at the track is, of course, the wheels. When new they are clean, and again, with the progress made over the years, they do not give the trouble they used to. A regular wipe with methylated spirit should keep them clean, but for anything tougher gentle application of a sharpened matchstick or small screwdriver tip should pick it off. Loco-motive wheels need the main attention because they directly affect running. There is, however, quite a backward and forward transfer of dirt between the other rolling stock wheels and the track, though here again improvements over the years have reduced the effect. At one time, the plastic wheels used seemed to attract dirt and after a while it became possible to peel the layer of dirt off. Recent metal wheels, or metal treads, have eased matters, but some plastic wheels have lately reappeared and only time will tell if the plastic used will have the same characteristic. When clean-ing wheels take the opportunity of making a check for true running.

With these precautions, everything should operate well, but even on the best-regulated layouts things are going to go wrong, due to time if nothing else. Loco-motives consist of working parts and that means wear. The main problem other than lubrication is likely to be lack of electrical continuity through the chassis and motor. Unless it is a hand-built chassis on the split-axle principle, there are going to be wiping contacts in some form on the wheels, and if your best locomotive is going along the track in a series of hiccups, the cause is more than likely to be dirt again. First check the track, especially if it always happens at the same place, and if that is all right the trouble is likely to be in the pickups. There should be at least two wheels being used for this purpose (there really can't be too many).

A power cleaning brush can be very useful. Fortunately it is not difficult to make one. The basis is a wire-bristle brush of the type sold for cleaning suede leather, looking rather like a large toothbrush. Divide the bristle head into half along its length and remove the centre row or two of bristles to make a gap about 6mm wide, then glue in a block of insulating material. It doesn't matter what it is, but sponge rubber is probably best. Connect a wire to the bunch of bristles each side of the insulation and the other ends to a track supply. For locomotives with driving wheel drive and pickup the brush is just held to the wheels, with the insulation between them, and when the power is supplied via the bristles the wheels will be cleaned while running.

A growing number of locomotives use tender drive with locomotive pickup, and of course with these the power cleaning brush system won't work. The pickup wheels can be spun and cleaned by hand and the drive wheels made to turn by putting the power cleaning brush on the pickup wheels and holding the same rag used for track cleaning against the drive wheels. Avoid using fluffy rags, obviously.

Problems caused by misuse or acci-dental damage should be dealt with by a service dealer or the service department of the manufacturer. However the area around the motor armature can be looked after by the non-expert. Whichever type of drive is employed, there will be a seg-mented moving commutator with a pair of static brushes, the latter almost always of carbon. The brush shape may vary, but

For the few pennies it costs, and the few minutes it takes to make, a power cleaning brush is well worth while. Note that it is only suitable for connection to the track supply, both for the health of the locomotive and that of the user! Only occasional use should be necessary.

centre bristles removed, replaced by foam rubber

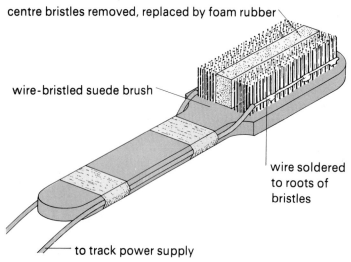

wire-bristled suede brush

wire soldered to roots of bristles

to track power supply

they will almost certainly be spring-loaded, either directly on to the brush or on to a metal arm (usually brass) carrying the carbon at one end. With a moving part in contact with a static one there will be wear, and periodic checking and servicing will repay with a much better-operating locomotive and therefore more enjoyment.

The instructions with the locomotive when new should explain how to take things apart so that this service can be carried out. The methylated spirit and rag will be needed again, together with a needle or pin, or better a sharp, wooden cocktail stick. Use the pin or stick to clean the narrow gaps between the segments of the commutator, being extremely careful to avoid damage, especially to the fine wires of the armature windings, the ends of which are attached to the segments. Next wipe the commutator with the methylated spirit-dampened rag, check the brushes for wear and if necessary replace.

All the above comments are of a general nature but they apply to almost all commercial models. Little or no trouble will be experienced if the manufacturers' instructions and a little common sense are used. Modern proprietary models are getting nearer to precision instruments every year and, apart from routine service, they are best left alone unless you are sure what you are doing.

Even while preparing this chapter a neighbour approached with his grandson's train, complaining that the driving wheels would not go right round. Long before his story was ended it was a fair guess that someone had been tampering with the valve gear and had reassembled it incorrectly, and this was so. Correction of the assembly and a little service on the pickups and the locomotive will give pleasure for many more hours.

Simple fault check list

In each case it is assumed that the locomotive is sitting on a track connected to a power supply via a transformer/controller.

1 Locomotive fails to move when controller is moved.
  Check electrical connections from mains plug through to track. Are all wheels on track? Remove power for short time to check automatic cut-out. If possible try another locomotive. Break track layout into small units starting from power input rail, reconnect working away from here until fault reappears.

2 Locomotive moves short distance then comes to a halt.
  Return a short distance and try again. Check track connections. Clean track.
3 Locomotive moves short distance then slows.
  Check track connections.
4 Locomotive does not run smoothly.
  Clean track. Clean wheels. Clean and reset pickups.
5 Any of above still applying after checks.
  Strip locomotive and clean commutator. Check and if necessary replace brushes.
6 Locomotive moves very slowly even on full power.
  As for 5. Have motor (in some cases complete chassis) remagnetised. (Never remove magnet without keeper plate—if in doubt leave alone.)
7 Any other faults.
  Best left to service dealer or someone who *knows* what he is doing.

If you thought that the chapter on track wiring exaggerated wire-tracing problems, imagine trying to locate a fault in the wiring of a control panel like this without some means of identification of the wires. Systematic, one-step-at-a-time checks are the only way to establish go and no-go situation faults.

NEW DEVELOPMENTS

Like many other hobbies, model railways have their 'optional extras' or luxury items which can be added. Some of the accessories on the market are most interesting and add extra enjoyment while others could almost be termed expensive novelties. It is very much a matter of personal choice and budget as to which accessories have the most appeal.

This consul is one of the first microchip controllers which can be expected to play an increasing part in future model railways. Inset is a photograph of the microchip control stations being fitted to the track.

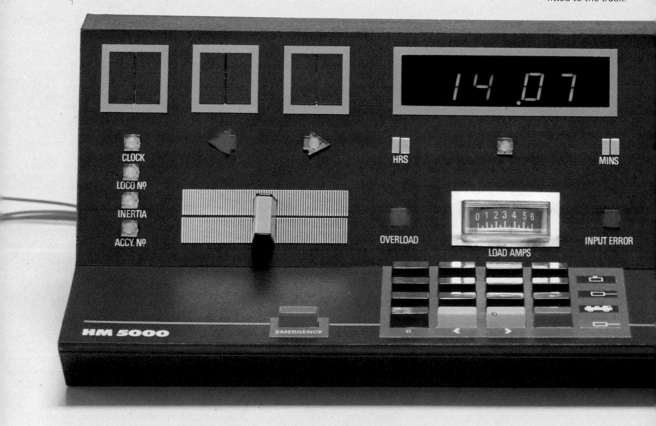

Smoke units

A unit can be fitted into certain types of locomotives which will produce smoke coming out of the chimney. The principle is simple; oil is fed into a small reservoir in the unit. This oil drops on to an electrically heated wire or plate and the resultant burning produces the smoke! Some units are worked by a small piston, mechanically driven from the axle, so that the smoke appears in puffs and the volume is roughly synchronised with the speed. Other types have a continual drift of smoke all the time. On some Hornby locomotives, smoke units are a standard feature. One of the best units is by Seuthe, which is made in West Germany but readily available in other countries. The smoke is non-toxic, but it is worth remembering that a small amount of oil will produce quite a lot of smoke.

Fibre optics

These are a very useful way of lighting small buildings, signs, lamps and signals in a realistic manner. The fibre optic is a length of flexible, clear plastic rod or filament which can be obtained in varying diameters. It will transmit light along its length which will then be visible at the end. A length of fibre optic placed in front of a small bulb (usually 12-volt/3 amp) will transmit light and illuminate the whole of the diameter of the end of the optic. A bunch of fibre optics can be lit by one small bulb and individual fibres can be led to various items such as station lamps, buildings and even signals. If a piece of coloured plastic is placed over the end of the fibre nearest to the light source, then that colour will show at the other end. Alternatively, a coloured bulb can be used but this will then illuminate every fibre being fed from that bulb with that particular colour. Fibre optics are fairly inexpensive and can be purchased from specialist shops in varying thickness, the larger the diameter, the greater the light given off.

Electric track cleaning

It is important that the rails and the locomotive wheels are kept clean. These are the means of transmitting the current and the voltage will not readily pass through a barrier of dirt on either the rails or the locomotive wheels. An alternative to cleaning the track by hand with a rag soaked in white spirit or methylated spirit is to use a high frequency generator unit. When the 12-volt track supply is interrupted, the unit generates a high frequency AC voltage which is superimposed upon the ordinary current. This burns away the dirt, ionises the gap, and the DC current then continues as normal. These small units are easily connected between the controller and the track and are automatic in operation. They can, however, cause severe interference with FM radio if a set is in use nearby. There are two makes currently on the market, Relco and Hammant & Morgan.

Sound systems

Many enthusiasts feel that to complete the atmosphere of a model railway there should be the sound of the trains, diesel or steam, rather than the hum from the electric motor. There are several ways of reproducing the sound; one of the easiest is to play a recording, feeding the output to small loudspeakers placed under the baseboard. However, this cannot be

synchronised with the movement of the model. Electronic synthesised sound units can be purchased which are coupled to the controller and the requisite signal (usually referred to as 'white noise') is superimposed on the track voltage. This is then picked up by a collector on the locomotive or tender and fed to a small loudspeaker which is normally housed in the tender. Perfect synchronisation is achieved and the sound can be quite realistic, but such units are not cheap. There is another problem, the locomotive or tender must have enough space to house the loudspeaker. It could, of course, be fitted into a coach or goods van, but then this would have to be permanently coupled to the locomotive.

Remote controlled uncoupling
There are two main methods of operating a remote uncoupling system. The first is to have a small ramp between the rails which can be raised or lowered by means of a mechanical lever or an electric relay. The wagons then pass over the ramp and when

it is in the raised position, the droppers on the coupling hooks are lifted so that they are clear of the bar on the adjacent wagon. The other method is to have an electro-magnet which is energised by a switch when the appropriate wagons are over the spot where uncoupling normally takes place. A special type of coupling using iron hooks (or droppers) has to be used and this type is not fitted to proprietary rolling stock by the manufacturers.

Electric point motors
Some proprietary points can be purchased with an electric point motor already attached and it is only necessary to connect the wires. Point motors are normally purchased separately and these units can be fitted alongside the point or placed underneath the baseboard; in either case they must be mechanically coupled to the tie-bar of the point. The point motor is really a solenoid, though sometimes points are operated by relays. Normally the current is not kept supplied to the point motor, as it merely needs a pulse to make it

Track-cleaning vehicles are now available, disguised as conventional rolling stock and thus able to circulate with a conventional train. The modern alternative is an automatic generator connected between controller and track which deals immediately with any dirt interrupting the current supply.

Lighting trains and track and running with the main room lights switched off adds a new dimension. Fibre optics facilitate this—for example, all signals can be operated from one light source—but small bulbs, called 'grain of wheat' size, are probably still the easiest way of lighting carriages.

work. Some motors take quite a high current, but as this is only a momentary flash (or passing contact on the operating switch) there is no danger of a burn-out. One popular method of operating the point motors is via an 'electric pencil'. A condensed track plan of the layout is drawn out on a piece of wood or board and brass screws inserted at the tracks leading from the points. The screws are then connected to the point motors with suitable wire; a wire is also run from the supply to a metal pencil and the other polarity direct to the point. Thus when the pencil or probe is touched onto the brass screw it makes the contact and energises the point motor accordingly. One can easily select the route for the train by running the electric pencil over the track diagram. The addition of a capacity discharge unit (a large condenser) will double the energy, in a quick burst, to the point motor and can be a worthwhile addition.

Electronic and transistorised controllers

The conventional controller is, in effect, a variable resistance which increases the voltage to the track as it is turned forward and thus permits the electric motor in the locomotive or 'prime mover' to go faster. Many electric motors require more volts to start than they do to run, and this is why one can often see a model locomotive start off at an unrealistically high speed. Some controllers do offer a half-wave rectification and this is virtually a pulsed start which will enable the locomotive to move away slowly. However, when the locomotive needs more power, such as when pulling a heavy train up a gradient, the variable resistance controller is often lacking. A variable transformer type has an advantage as it will give more power,

flexible lead and either run off the main controller as an extension to same, or is plugged into the layout at a convenient point. It is extremely useful on large layouts, especially those where the operator cannot see all his tracks from the normal control position. With the ECM Rambler type he can set and control his train from the main position, then move to another part of the layout, plug in his hand-held module and continue to control the train from the remote position.

Command control

Sometimes referred to as a two-wire system, this very advanced form of electronic control was introduced in 1979 by Hornby Hobbies and Airfix, with their Zero-1 and Multiple Train Control respectively. Unfortunately the two systems are not compatible in any way.

The big advantage of the system is that it will allow the operator to run up to four trains on the same track or on any part of the layout. There is no need for sectionalising the layout, so the mass of wires and switches are largely eliminated. Both systems use 20-volt AC (the normal track voltage for model railways is 12-volt DC) and the locomotives must be fitted with a module or 'chip' which then means it cannot be used with conventional locomotives on a normal layout; furthermore a model not fitted with a chip must in no circumstances be used on a layout that is operated by the Zero-1 or

but it is not as efficient as some of the more modern transistor controllers which incorporate electronic circuits which will automatically permit more power to be available and at the same time they will give a representation of the inertia and weight of the prototype with slow starting and stopping. They will often have facilities for a pre-determined delay so that speed is built up or decreased, plus the option of delayed braking to predetermined levels via a multi-way switch which will enable the operator to select the degree of braking. All these controls give much more realistic effect and all movements can be carefully controlled to scale proportions. There is also a greater element of skill in the operation using this type of controller.

Walk-round controls

This is a hand-held controller fitted onto a

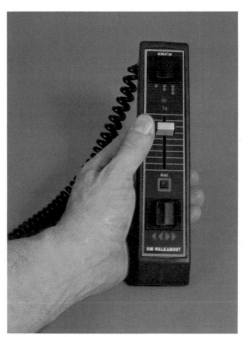

Below: The use of hand controllers or walk-round controls has become more common in the last year or two, probably because obtaining different viewpoints during running adds to the interest. Most control only one section of track at a time, and are therefore of most use on complete circuits.

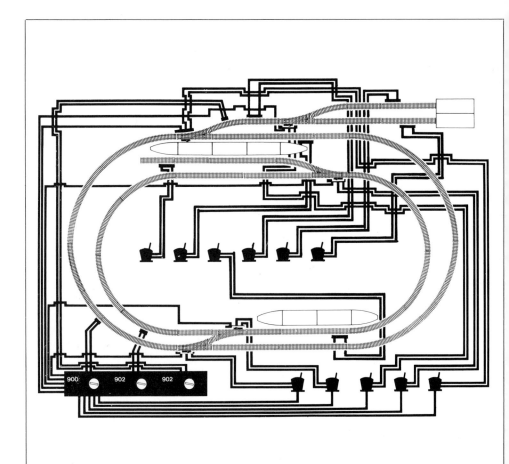

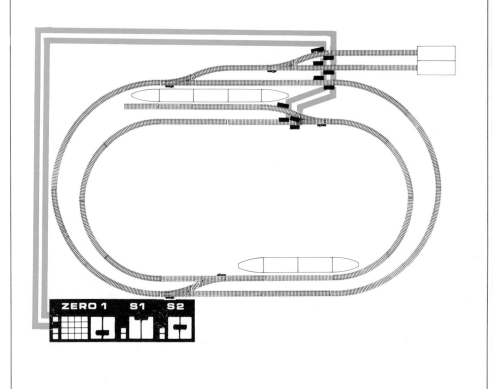

he Airfix MTC system.

The master controller contains a microprocessor and a keyboard not unlike an electronic calculator on which one 'calls up' the number code of the locomotive. In the Hornby system up to 16 locomotives can be operated with additional slave units attached to the main controller. When the number code has been passed to the locomotive it is then receiving the signals sent to it in respect of direction and speed, the latter being controlled like a normal controller but with slider type controls. If another locomotive is then wanted this is again called up and responds to the signals, while the first locomotive continues running according to its last received signal. It is not possible to control two simultaneously. The Hornby Zero-1 is a digital system with a square waveform which is interrupted for a microsecond to impart the signal. It is an excellent system for the control of points and can work up to 99 points or accessories merely by tapping out the corresponding number on the keyboard.

The Airfix Multiple Train Control also uses a module or chip, but of a different kind as this is tuned for four channels. Up to four locomotives can all be independently controlled on this system via the four walk-around type hand controllers which have sliding type switches for variations of speed and the usual toggle switch for change of direction.

At the time of writing there is not much technical information available on either system and extensions to both are still being planned. Another system is also coming on the market. This is a compromise between the Command Control system and the conventional controllers. This is the ECM Selectrol, which has the advantage that locomotives not fitted with chips will still run on the layout, although of course they will not be under the two-wire control.

The fast-moving technology of present day life will inevitably be reflected in model railways of the future but skill and enthusiasm will still bring the greatest rewards.

Opposite: The difference between the wiring needed for a conventional control system and a modern chip control such as Zero 1 is graphically illustrated. A disadvantage is that normal 12-volt DC locomotives cannot be run on the chip layout, nor chip locomotives on a standard 12-volt track.

Below: Computer-style techniques and terminology were bound to be introduced to model railways sooner or later; they hold few terrors for younger enthusiasts but, one suspects, there will continue to be period type layouts in which operation will still be carried out by what have become traditional methods.

SCALES

Gauge 1

Scale 10mm : 1ft   *Ratio* 1 : 32
Gauge 44.5mm or $1\frac{1}{4}$in
This is the size of the early railway models
and not a specialist scale. Models in this
size can be powered by live steam. Ideal for
garden railways, although little is available
commercially except for the LGB models
of narrow gauge and some standard gauge
prototype models from Marklin.

Gauge 0

Scale 7mm : 1ft   *Ratio* 1 : 45
Gauge 32mm
Prior to the Second World War this was
the most popular size. Several manufacturers deal with this gauge and it is ideal
for the garden, large shed or large room
indoors. Electricity is now the normal
method of propulsion, replacing clockwork, but live steam can also be used.
Older commercial models are usually
referred to as coarse scale, and have thick
wheels and deep flanges; the more modern
locos and rolling stock have finer standards. American railway modellers also
use this gauge but use a ratio of 1 : 48 with
a scale of $\frac{1}{4}$in : 1ft.

S gauge

Scale $\frac{3}{16}$in : 1ft   *Ratio* 1 : 65
Gauge 22.2mm
A size popular in America in the 1930s and
1940s, built by American Flyer from 1945–
1966. This is regarded as a specialist scale
in Great Britain. No commercial parts are
available.

Scalefour and Protofour

Scale 4mm : 1ft   *Ratio* 1 : 76
Gauge 18.83mm
This is the exact gauge for the scale. It is a
specialist size, although a few commercial
organisations produce parts only, and some
proprietary 00 equipment can be converted.

EM gauge

Scale 4mm : 1ft   *Ratio* 1 : 76
Gauge 18mm
EM means Eighteen Millimetre and is

nearer the true scale gauge than 00 for
4ft $8\frac{1}{2}$in prototype. Several firms produce
parts and it is usually quite easy to convert
proprietary models.

00 gauge

Scale 4mm : 1ft   *Ratio* 1 : 76
Gauge 16.5mm
00 is the most popular gauge in Great
Britain with the main proprietary manufacturers such as Airfix, Hornby, Lima and
Palitoy taking the lead. A vast number of
small firms produce kits, parts, accessories
and materials. Models are moderately
robust and it is the most economical size
with regard to money and the space
needed in relation to detail of model. It is
ideal for indoor use.

H0 scale

Scale 3.5mm : 1ft   *Ratio* 1 : 87
Gauge 16.5mm
This is the Continental and American size
and is the true scale for the track gauge.
There are few models for British outline,
but it is the universal size on the Continent
and in America.

TT gauge

Scale 3mm : 1ft   *Ratio* 1 : 101
Gauge 12mm
Commercially-produced by Tri-ang in the
late 1950s, it was discontinued as a proprietary product. A few firms produce parts
and kits, but it could now be classed as a
specialist scale. Continental firms make
models to a ratio of 1 : 120 at a scale of
2.5mm : 1ft.

N gauge

Scale 2.06mm : 1ft   *Ratio* 1 : 148
Gauge 9mm
First produced by Arnold (West Germany)
in the early 1960s, this size has become
popular in England as well as on the
Continent and in America. There are
several firms producing equipment, the
brand leaders in Great Britain being
Graham Farish and Peco. N gauge is ideal
for indoor use where space is limited, or

where the operator wishes to model scenery more than the building of locomotives etc. The Continental (and American) ratio is : 160 and scale of 1.91mm : 1ft.

Z gauge

Scale 1.5mm : 1ft   *Ratio* 1 : 220
Gauge 6.5mm

This is the smallest workable size. It is only produced by Marklin of West Germany. At the time of writing some English bodies may be produced for fitting to the Continental chassis.

Narrow gauges

These are variations of the above scales and gauges, and generally speaking, are for the more specialist or advanced modeller. There are some kits and loco-motives available in the most popular size of 00n9, which is 4mm : 1ft scale bodies, buildings and scenery but running on N gauge (9mm) track.

American Variations

The most popular scales in the U.S.A. are H0, N, 0, $H0_N3$ and 0_N3, the latter two being for narrow gauge enthusiasts. Much ready-to-run equipment is available in H0 and N, but in the others a considerable amount of hand-building is required. More use is made of 'can' motors, the short, stubby, almost fully-enclosed motors which were developed principally by the Japanese for electric slot cars, and they are sometimes used to drive a flywheel, giving slow starts and coasting stops to trains.

Another American innovation is NTRAK, a modular track system in N gauge in which the modules are each built by different individuals or clubs to laid-down standards, allowing quick and easy assembly of large and varied layouts at club meetings or area conventions. This approach has been taken up in several other countries, including England, and is growing in popularity.

TOOLS

What tools are required will depend on the approach to the subject. A full layout will obviously require basic normal carpentry tools and those required for scenic work tend to be self-evident. Finer implements are needed when rolling stock, buildings and locomotives are constructed and some suggestions are shown here. There are substitutes for some of the more expensive items such as the vernier gauge; basically much can be done with knife, rule, razor saw, fine screwdrivers and pliers, files and small drills. Buy as the need arises is a sensible maxim for the average modeller.

GLOSSARY

adhesive weight proportion of locomotive weight borne by driving wheels.

aqueduct structure carrying water over depressed ground.

armature wire-wound rotating bobbin core of electric motors used in models.

ash trolley wheeled container running on narrow rails between and beneath normal rails for removal of locomotive clinker and ash.

ballast chippings spread between and around sleepers.

Belpaire type of flat-topped firebox on locomotive.

block train train made up of identical wagons or vans etc.

Bo-Bo diesel or electric locomotive having two driven axles, i.e. four driving wheels, on each of two bogies.

bogie a swivelling assembly carrying usually four wheels (sometimes six) mounted below a locomotive or coach.

bolster principal cross-member of a bogie carrying the pivot.

brake van usually the last vehicle in a train from which the guard (conductor) can operate the train's brakes if necessary.

buffers strongly sprung shock-absorbing fittings at each end of all railway vehicles.

bunker coal receptacle at rear of tank locomotive.

cab control separation of layout into independently-controlled blocks.

caboose U.S. equivalent of guard's van/ brake van.

can motor electric motor with side magnets enclosed in thin metal box, developed originally for slot car racing.

carriage common English term for passenger coach.

cascading down gradual relegation of wearing rolling stock to less demanding or prestigious uses.

catenary arrangement of suspended wires for overhead current collection.

centre-swing the overhang of the centre of a long vehicle on the inside of a sharp bend.

chairs iron castings spiked to sleepers (ties) to secure rails.

clerestory roof roof with central vertical extension the sides of which are glazed.

coach vehicle for accommodation of passengers (car in U.S.).

Co-Co locomotive with three driving axles (six wheels) on each bogie.

collector contact rubbing on live rail or wire to pass electricity.

commutator contact ring on armature shaft split into segments corresponding to number of windings, receiving current from brushes.

concertina connection U.S. term for bellows gangway between coaches.

conductor U.S. equivalent of guard, in charge of train.

coupling device for connecting vehicles into train.

crossover pointwork allowing a train to divert to a parallel line.

crosstie longer than standard sleeper (tie) beneath points etc.

cutting excavated channel through rise of ground.

decal printed lettering or design which can be transferred to vehicle.

diaphragm gangway another term for bellows or concertina connection.

dome fitting on top of boiler from which steam is led to cylinders.

double-acting steam engine where steam is applied alternately to either side of piston(s).

double-decker coach etc with accommodation on two levels.

double-heading connection of two locomotives to one train.

double-slip point complex point allowing crossing other lines with additional rail allowing train to move on to one of several tracks.

dribbler early trackless steam locomotive model.

dump wagon type of wagon body which can be tilted to discharge load.

electric pencil conductive rod used for quick closing of electric circuits.

embankment built-up track base over dip in ground.

end-swing overhang of long vehicle ends on sharp curve.

engineer U.S. term for engine-driver.

fiddle-yard area of layout, often concealed, where trains can be made up manually etc.

fishplate connector between ends of lengths of rail holding ends firmly in alignment; sometimes erroneously relied on for electrical connection.

flash extraneous material on moulding where dies were not sufficiently tight together.

flatcar platform wagon for self-supporting loads.

footplate locomotive platform for driver and fireman.

freight car U.S. term for goods van (also boxcar).

frog break in rail permitting wheels to cross (in pointwork).

ganger railway employee engaged on upkeep of track.

gauge the actual width, centre to centre, between rails.

gondola car U.S. platform wagon fitted with low sides.

goods train train carrying materials, produce etc. (U.S. freight train)

gradient slope or incline, usually expressed as a ratio, e.g. 1 : 120.

guard official responsible for train, other than driving.

half-wave rectification electronic means of controlling current supply allowing very precise control and full power irrespective of speed.

head shunt trackwork allowing a locomotive to move away after pulling a train into a terminal platform.

hornhook a type of non-scale coupling, reasonably simple to operate.

interlocking tower U.S. term for signal box.

island site layout area allowing operator to walk round all sides.

jumper cables free-ended multi-strand electrical cables plugged in when portable sectionalised tracks are reassembled.

ladder arrangement of parallel rows of sidings.

leading wheels carrying wheels ahead of driving wheels on locomotive.

livery consistent colour scheme employed by railway to identify/publicise their locomotives and other rolling stock, vehicles etc.

loading gauge the physical dimensions which will pass safely through tunnels, past other trains etc of a specific railway, also the light metal frame suspended from an arm which checks dimensions.

microchips minute integrated electronic circuits.

monitor roof raised central roof extension like a clerestory but without windows.

motive power depot complex for servicing and readying locomotives.

multiple aspect signals electric light signals (red, amber, green).

observation car passenger coach with extra facilities for viewing scenery.

open platform end form of passenger car with railed balcony at rear.

pannier tank tank locomotive carrying water supply in side tanks.

pantograph sprung frame used for current collection from overhead wires.

pilot engine locomotive used (usually) at terminal station for handling empty coaches and so on.

pilot truck U.S. term for leading bogie (truck) on locomotive.

points (U.S. turn-outs or switches) trackwork allowing a train to change from one set of lines to another or proceed in either of two directions.

pony truck two wheeled swivelling assembly ahead of or behind locomotive driving wheels.

Pullman passenger coach with dining facilities and comfortable seats.

queen-post vertical strut supporting wagon/coach substructure.

railbus type of (usually) two-car train running regular local services.

railcar as railbus in countries other than Britain.

rake set of coaches made up into a train or part of one.

rating plan scale drawing of an area of railway including all buildings, basically for calculation of rates (local taxes) payable.

reception road track for goods trains leading into (but stopping at) station for handling parcels, mails and so on.

release crossover pointwork near end of rails in terminus to allow locomotive to depart leaving train at platform.

reverse loop loop of track returning locomotive to original line in opposite direction, requiring current polarity to be reversed.

rolling resistance the drag of a vehicle or train opposing tractive effort.

saddle tank a tank engine carrying water supply in a tank fitted and curved over the top of the boiler.

scale the relationship between any dimension of a model and that of its full-size counterpart.

semaphore signal the older type of signal employing a counterbalanced arm, the position of which instructs a driver.

shunting (U.S. switching) the arrangement of vehicles into a train.

shunting engine locomotive used to manoeuvre coaches, wagons and so on, to make up a train in the correct sequence.

shunting neck track(s) leading into a marshalling area in which they debouch into a number of sidings.

side tanks water containers mounted on either side of a tank engine boiler.

sidings tracks of limited length adjacent to main lines, used for shunting, loading/ unloading or temporary vehicle storage.

signal box a control centre for all signals affecting a particular stretch of line (U.S. interlocking tower).

single-slip type of point allowing crossing or travel on alternative track.

six-foot way the area between pairs of main lines.

sleeper heavy wood, sometimes concrete, cross-member supporting track (U.S. tie). Also passenger car with sleeping accommodation.

solebar main fore and aft joist each side of wagon frame.

spectacle plate front of locomotive driving cab with small windows.

splasher casing concealing upper part of locomotive driving wheels.

spline flexible strip of wood or metal used to draw curves.

Standard gauge American gauge of $2\frac{1}{4}$in used in 1906, now obsolete.

station throat point from which main lines spread into several platforms.

strapping metal strip reinforcement on wagon or van body.

stretcher cross-member between locomotive or bogie frames.

stud metal connection in centre of each sleeper contacting a wiper beneath locomotive for electrical pick-up, now rarely seen. Also a collection of locomotives.

superelevation banking of track in tight curves by raising outside rail.

tank locomotive one carrying water and coal supplies on one chassis.

tender locomotive one drawing a separate vehicle (the tender) carrying coal and water supplies in greater quantities.

tie U.S., see sleeper.

towerman U.S. term for signalman manning signal box (interlocking tower).

trailer coach unpowered second part of a railcar or railbus.

trammel instrument for describing large-radius curves.

transfers original English term for decals (q.v.).

tread the horizontal (actually very slightly coned) face of a locomotive tyre.

truss rod diagonal brace in underframe of a wagon for example.

turn-out see point.

turret similar to dome, a fitting on the top of a boiler for steam feed.

underlay slightly resilient base material on which model track is laid.

valve gear linkage controlling steam admission to cylinders.

van closed goods vehicle (U.S. boxcar).

ventilation tower brick structure for ventilating tunnel beneath.

viaduct elevated structure carrying road and/or railway across valley.

weathering technique of painting simulating normal wear and tear.

wheel arrangement disposition of driving and carrying wheels on a locomotive.

Whyte notation widely used description of wheel arrangement using numbers of carrying, driving and carrying wheels listed front to rear. Certain common arrangements are referred to by names, e.g. Atlantic 4-4-2, Baltic 4-6-4, Consolidation 2-8-0, Mikado 2-8-2, Mogul 2-6-0, Pacific 4-6-2, Prairie 2-6-2 and so on.

INDEX

(T) signifies trade name.

Acknowledgements

The publishers would like to thank all the institutions and individuals, both in the U.K. and overseas, who have helped with photographs and information, in particular
Hammant & Morgan Ltd.,
Handem Works, Apem Estate,
St Albans Road, Watford, Herts.

Victors (Model Railways) Ltd.,
166 Pentonville Road, London N.1.

John Piper of Scalelink.

Hornby Hobbies Ltd., Margate.

Rolf Ertmer 30, 34, 35, 43, 46, 47, 48, 64, Hammant and Morgan 50, 51, Robert Hegge 2, 3, 6, 7, 64, 74, 102, 103, 107, 174, Hornby 8, 22, 27, 177, Nelson Twells 93, John Wylie 4, 6, 7, 10, 11, 13, 15, 18, 19, 21, 38, 45, 62, 63, 67, 68, 69, 70, 72, 76, 78, 79, 83, 84, 88, 89, 90, 91, 94, 96, 97, 99, 100, 104, 105, 106, 108, 109, 110, 111, 112, 113, 114, 115, 116, 117, 118, 119, 120, 121, 122, 123, 124, 125, 126, 128, 129, 130, 137, 144, 146, 147, 150, 151, 154, 155, 156, 157, 158, 159, 160, 161, 162, 163, 166, 169, 173, 180